Marc E. Vargo, MS

Noble Lives
Biographical Portraits of Three Remarkable Gay Men— Glenway Wescott, Aaron Copland, and Dag Hammarskjöld

More pre-publication
REVIEWS, COMMENTARIES, EVALUATIONS . . .

"Mark E. Vargo's book has introduced a brilliant new subgenre.
These concise yet thoroughly researched
biographies make an important contribution to history and scholarship. Vargo's energetic, vibrant descriptions bring
his subjects to life. More than that,
his writing invigorates the pages of this
book and gives the reader a full, rounded
sense of Wescott, Copland, and Hammarskjöld—not simply as talented individuals but as adventurers who each, in
his own way, successfully navigated the
dangerous and exciting terrain of twentieth-century gay life. Vargo has created a
rare and wonderful thing—a book that is
an utter pleasure to consume even as it
remains solid in its scholarly complexity
and depth."

Dennis Denisoff, PhD
Author of *The Winter Gardeners*

"Vargo's three biographies create
an occasion for reflection that has
a value that far exceeds the value of any
one life; yet its existence depends on
each individual. On one level, this well-
written book is an effective introduc-
tion to three lesser-known figures of
contemporary gay history; on another
level, it is a metaphor powerful enough
to prompt reflection on our commitment to the individual as the basis of
social order—or our lack thereof."

Greg Bredbeck, PhD
Professor, Department of English,
University of California, Riverside

HPP

Harrington Park Press®
An Imprint of The Haworth Press, Inc.
New York • London • Oxford

Noble Lives
Biographical Portraits
of Three Remarkable Gay Men—
Glenway Wescott,
Aaron Copland,
and Dag Hammarskjöld

Harrington Park Press®
Titles of Related Interest

Noble Lives
Biographical Portraits
of Three Remarkable Gay Men—
Glenway Wescott,
Aaron Copland,
and Dag Hammarskjöld

Marc E. Vargo, MS

HPP

Harrington Park Press®
An Imprint of The Haworth Press, Inc.
New York • London • Oxford

For more information on this book or to order, visit
http://www.haworthpress.com/store/product.asp?sku=5401

or call 1-800-HAWORTH (800-429-6784) in the United States and Canada
or (607) 722-5857 outside the United States and Canada

or contact orders@HaworthPress.com

Published by

Harrington Park Press®, an imprint of The Haworth Press, Inc., 10 Alice Street, Binghamton, NY 13904-1580.

Cover design by Marylouise E. Doyle.

Cover photo credits:

Photo of Glenway Wescott by Carl Van Vechten, from the Yale Collection of American Literature, Beinecke Rare Book and Manuscript Library, reprinted with permission from the Van Vechten Trust.

Photo of Aaron Copland by Victor Kraft, reprinted with permission from Rheba Kraft.

Photo of Dag Hammarskjöld reprinted courtesy of United Nations/Department of Public Information.

Library of Congress Cataloging-in-Publication Data

Vargo, Marc.
    Noble lives : biographical portraits of three remarkable gay men—Glenway Wescott, Aaron Copland, and Dag Hammarskjöld / Marc E. Vargo.
        p. cm.
    Includes bibliographical references and index.
    ISBN: 1-56023-294-3 (hard : alk. paper)
    ISBN: 1-56023-545-4 (soft : alk. paper)
    1. Wescott, Glenway, 1901- 2. Copland, Aaron, 1900- 3. Hammarskjöld, Dag, 1905-1961.
4. Gay men—Biography. 5. Authors, American—20th century—Biography. 6. Composers—United States—Biography. 7. Statesmen—Sweden—Biography. I. Title.

HQ75.7.V37 2005
306.76'62'092273—dc22

2004014892

CONTENTS

ABOUT THE AUTHOR

Marc E. Vargo, MS, is a staff member in the Active Treatment Department (Psychological Services) at Hammond Developmental Center in Hammond, Louisiana. He is the author of *Scandal: Infamous Gay Controversies of the Twentieth Century, Acts of Disclosure: The Coming-Out Process of Contemporary Gay Men,* and *The HIV Test: What You Need to Know to Make an Informed Decision.* His work has also appeared in the Italian journal *Cortex,* the *British Journal of Medical Psychology,* the *Journal of the American Academy of Behavioral Medicine, Psychological Reports,* and the *Journal of Clinical Psychology.* He lives in New Orleans, Louisiana.

Acknowledgments

My gratitude goes to all those at The Haworth Press who were a part of this project, with special thanks to Josh Ribakove for his help with this and previous books. I also appreciate the generous assistance of Carmen Fernandez at Thirteen/WNET New York (PBS), as well as the judicious advice of my agent Pamela Gray Ahearn in New Orleans. Above all, I'm grateful to Michael, Molly, and Jillian, whose warmth and wit kept me in fine spirits during the writing of this book.

Nearly all men can withstand adversity; if you want to test a man's character, give him power.

Abraham Lincoln

Prologue

In the course of the twentieth century, scores of talented men and women made vital contributions to the fields of science, religion, politics, and the arts and, in so doing, made the world a finer place for us all. Among the ranks of such notables we find an impressive roster of names, from Albert Schweitzer to Albert Einstein, from Marie Curie to Martin Luther King; courageous, committed individuals whose actions benefited society at large.

In *Noble Lives: Biographical Portraits of Three Remarkable Gay Men,* three such figures are revisited: Glenway Wescott, the expatriate Jazz Age author who wrote incisively about life in the American heartland; Aaron Copland, the Academy Award–winning composer whose music captured the essence of the American spirit; and Dag Hammarskjöld, the Swedish economist, Nobel laureate, and Secretary-General of the United Nations who struggled tirelessly to preserve global peace during the early years of the Cold War.

These three men shared not only a distinctive brilliance and widespread popular acclaim but also an amalgam of personality characteristics. They were all rather humble, for instance, as well as self-effacing and reserved. By necessity they learned to contend with profound public visibility, including the searing scrutiny of the media.

Another mutual feature was their respect for, and goodwill toward, their colleagues. Despite the enormous strides these men made in the course of their distinguished careers, each earned and retained the admiration and affection of his peers throughout his lifetime.

Still another common trait was their affinity for other men, or an apparent affinity in the case of Dag Hammarskjöld. All three came of age during the first half of the twentieth century, an era during which same-sex love was disdained in Europe and North America. This was a time when people in high-profile positions, regardless of their sexual desires, were expected to marry in a demonstration of respect for, and an adherence to, social convention. Wescott, Copland, and Hammarskjöld refused to engage in such subterfuge, instead maintaining their integrity in spite of considerable social pressure to do otherwise.

Specifically, Wescott and Copland lived openly with their male lovers, while Hammarskjöld appears to have opted for abstinence.

One final similarity pertains to their legacies. Although the world was enhanced by the extraordinary contributions of these three prodigies, it seems that the men themselves are being forgotten. Today, many people have never heard of Glenway Wescott, and Dag Hammarskjöld's name has long since faded from public discourse. Even the details of Aaron Copland's life are becoming obscured, although his reputation endures and his compositions continue to be performed around the world. It is imperative that the human faces behind the remarkable deeds be examined, most notably the unique combination of talent and traits that allowed these men to attain such heights in the course of their lifetimes. Not only do they deserve such remembrance, but society will benefit by rediscovering the meaning of true brilliance at a time when it is marked by an unsavory obsession with shallow and fleeting celebrity.

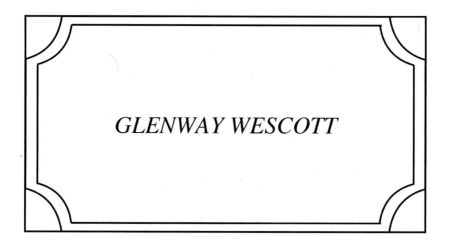

GLENWAY WESCOTT

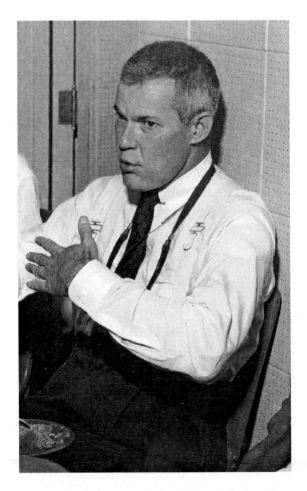

Glenway Wescott at the Institute for Sex Research, Indiana University, 1952. (Photo by William Dellenback. Reprinted with permission from The Kinsey Institute for Research in Sex, Gender, and Reproduction.)

INTRODUCTION

In 1940, Glenway Wescott published *The Pilgrim Hawk,* a novel that enjoyed sweeping praise upon its release and a work that Susan Sontag in more recent times hailed as "astonishing . . . among the treasures of twentieth-century American literature."[1] Despite its merit many people today are unaware of this literary classic and of Wescott himself, although he was one of the finest writers of his day. His books, although superb in quality, were scarce in quantity, thereby causing him to lack the impressive canon of works boasted by his friends and colleagues Somerset Maugham, Colette, and E. M. Forster. Wescott, perfectionistic to the extreme, found it nearly impossible to complete a book-length manuscript, even though the few he did finish were truly outstanding, winning critical acclaim and inspiring future generations of writers.

Wescott's personal life was as remarkable as his literary creations. Never one to conceal his sexual orientation, he conducted himself as an openly gay man at a time when few other public figures dared to do so. Shortly after he published his groundbreaking saga of pioneer life, *The Grandmothers,* in 1927, he could be found living in France with two other men in a very visible ménage à trois, a bond that endured for the next two decades. Certainly his life was as original as any tale he ever devised in print, that of an internationally celebrated, but frequently blocked, author whose colorful life began on a farm in the American Midwest.

This biographical account follows Wescott's childhood and adolescence in rural Wisconsin, his student years at the University of Chicago, his stint at an artist's colony in Santa Fe, and his stretch as an expatriate writer in France during the Jazz Age. Also examined are his deeds as a politically active citizen of the United States during the buttoned-down 1950s, including his involvement with the CIA-sponsored Congress for Cultural Freedom, and his work with Alfred Kinsey at Indiana University's famed Institute for Sex Research. The aim is to achieve a better understanding of this complex, conscientious, and compassionate artist, a man whose literary and political contributions to American life deserve remembrance and appreciation.

3

WISCONSIN DAYS

Born April 11, 1901, in the small town of Kewaskum, Wisconsin, Glenway Wescott entered the world in humble circumstances. Although his family's farm was average in size, his weary, hardworking father was unable to afford any livestock other than pigs, thereby limiting the scope of the business from the start. Worsening matters was the location itself; situated at the base of a hill, several acres were prone to flooding. The farming operation was further hindered by the composition of the family. Of the Wescott's six children, four were girls and thus were considered unsuited to hard labor. As a result, life for the family was far from pleasant, including that of young Glenway, who was said to have been "too sensitive" for rustic living.[2] Certainly it was evident that he was no farm boy and had no intention of becoming one. As a child who sang soprano, prodded his elderly neighbors into telling him Indian tales, and found the Book of Leviticus scandalous and therefore enjoyable reading, his overarching aim was to exchange his dreary existence for a brighter, more vibrant one. He began to attain this goal at the age of twelve, when he left the family farm, along with the town's one-room schoolhouse, to attend high school in nearby West Bend, Wisconsin.

In this larger city, Wescott boarded with a Methodist minister and took his meals at rooming houses and with relatives. He also took an interest in his schoolwork, studying diligently and writing the occasional story for his school's newspaper. Then, when he was thirteen years old, he had an experience that proved indelible: during a sleep-over in which he shared a bed with two other boys, he had sex with one of the youths while the third boy dozed. Years later, Wescott would speculate that this experience, his first erotic encounter, may well have been responsible for his lifelong penchant for threesomes. He would also use his young lover and himself as the basis for characters in a 1928 short story, "Adolescence." He and his boyfriend remained attached for nearly two years, their relationship coming to a close only after the latter announced his desire to begin dating girls. Predictably, given this was Wescott's first love, he took their breakup so hard that he did not become involved with another young man until five years later, after he had graduated from high school and completed three semesters at the University of Chicago.

"I was small . . . I was homosexual. I was poor," writes Wescott, describing himself as a college freshman.[3] Sixteen years old at the time of admission and a scholarship student, he lived in a leafy Chicago neighborhood with wealthy friends of the family. He did not feel welcome in their opulent home, nor did he feel accepted by his classmates at the university. Chatty and effeminate, he sensed that he did not belong anywhere. Fortunately, his prospects began to change when he met fellow student Yvor Winters, the son of a wealthy stockbroker and a promising young man who became a leading force in the Imagist poetry movement of the 1920s. Winters took Wescott under his wing, introducing him to a clique of talented young writing students and urging him to join the university's Poetry Club. Wescott eagerly complied and found the elite club to his liking, describing it as "a snobbish, impassionated, and clever group of young poets."[4] Before long, he was elected president of the group due to his impressive organizational skills and proficiency as a public speaker.

Wescott did not have a burning interest in poetry, although he did develop an appreciation of imagist verse and became a passable poet himself given his age. Still, his adeptness notwithstanding, with further experience he came to realize that he preferred creating longer, less formal works. Years later he would even question whether training himself to meticulously compose verse had been a mistake, whether it had hampered his subsequent efforts as a novelist.

Wescott said,

> I myself began as a poet, which is a not altogether advantageous background for a life of fiction writing. The art of poetry is word by word, in very close connections like lace, juxtapositions like mosaic. Whereas to tell a story as it should be told, especially a long story or a novel, we must cast an easier spell, looser and farther flung.[5]

In spite of his growing attraction to fiction, Wescott had no plans to become a professional author, at least not at this early stage. The idea of a literary career occurred to him only after a friend told him, a few years later, that life as a gay man would be easier if he were an artist, that society would be more tolerant of his sexual orientation. The upshot: "I proceeded to become a writer," Wescott said.[6]

His sex life was apparently nonexistent while he attended college, in part because he became involved in a platonic romance with Kathlene

Foster, a fellow Poetry Club member whose fiancé had been killed in World War I. Wescott forged a strong, sympathetic relationship with this woman, trying vainly to fall in love with her and even proposing marriage at one point. In time, though, his thoughts drifted back to men. He also took a painfully close look at his own life at this time, especially when he found it necessary to quit school because he had contracted a debilitating illness.

In 1919, the gifted young writer was diagnosed with the Spanish flu, a pernicious ailment that killed more Americans in a single year than the combined domestic death tolls of the Vietnam War, the Korean War, and both World Wars.[7] The condition required Wescott to be hospitalized on two occasions and left him weak and dispirited. Unfortunately, during his prolonged convalescence he was able to do little more than reflect on his circumstances and examine his future prospects, a process that caused him great discouragement. It was in this disconcerted state that he made a halfhearted suicide attempt—he ran full-speed through the streets until he collapsed in a gutter—a desperate act triggered by his distress about being gay. Shortly after this incident he met the person who was to become his lifelong soul mate, Monroe Wheeler, a handsome, cultivated man two years his senior. Among other benefits, Wheeler helped Wescott accept his same-sex orientation and fostered his development as a writer during the decades that followed.

The two men forged an unconventional relationship marked by intermittent love affairs. When Wescott began dating Wheeler, for instance, Wheeler was still romancing women, a situation that persisted for some time and one that both men accepted without a hitch. In later years, Wescott disclosed that their sex life had always been lukewarm, that their bond, from the start, had been more intellectual than physical. If this were the case, it would help explain why their relationship endured for such a long time and withstood so many career-related separations. Such absences were surely frequent over the years and seemed to do no harm to their union, the first of which took place only a few months after they met and fell in love.

At that time, Yvor Winters, Wescott's former college friend, invited Wescott to move to Santa Fe, New Mexico. Winters had relocated to the desert city to recover from tuberculosis, and, once there, had become enchanted with its renowned artists' colony. Convinced that Wescott would appreciate it too, he extended his invitation. Wescott found the idea very appealing, especially since he was still in poor health himself and could use the change in climate. Further sweetening the deal, Winters' rich father, who was under the mistaken impression that Wescott would be helping his son recuperate from tuberculosis, offered to cover the writer's expenses. On this pretext Wescott made his way to Santa Fe, where he lived for nearly a year while honing his writing skills. It was also a time when he set out to make interesting new acquaintances, a venture that produced mixed results.

"I was too good-looking, too pretty . . . and very flamboyant," Wescott has said about his New Mexico period. "Some people adored me, and others got irritated."[8] Apparently, some also considered him scandalous. In his excellent account of the writer's life, biographer Jerry Rosco explains that Wescott took into his small Santa Fe home a sensual young Scandinavian man who had studied at the prestigious Art Institute of Chicago and was serving as an artist's apprentice and carpenter in the New Mexico city. Impoverished, he was living in the basement of a partially constructed house. Wescott, moved by the young man's plight as well as by his blond beauty, invited him to share his home and his bed. For the next several weeks, moreover, Wescott and the Scandinavian, who was strictly heterosexual, slept together—and nothing else—a platonic arrangement that frustrated Wescott. This was not the end of it, however. Adding to the illusion of impropriety, one of Wescott's friends from Chicago arrived on the scene and moved into a spare room in the tiny house, thereby creating the impression of a ménage à trois. In this way, Wescott found himself ensconced, innocently enough, in yet another "triangle," as he described it, a situation the townspeople considered risqué.[9]

Finally, after a lengthy stay in Santa Fe during which Wescott renewed his health, improved his writing skills, and befriended a handful of artistic and literary luminaries, he returned to the Midwest and to the embrace of Monroe Wheeler. Wescott was heartened by their reunion and was further pleased to learn that, during his absence, his lover had at last settled on a career. Specifically, Wheeler wished to immerse himself in the publishing process and had decided to begin by releasing a collection of Wescott's poems. It was in this way that *The Bitterns* was published in 1921.

As could be expected, the young writer was thrilled to see his work in print, signifying that he was a bona fide author. The reviews that followed, however, were few in number and mixed in content. At issue was the excessive melancholy that infused his work, causing some readers to regard it as "juvenilia" and as "the lyric outcries of youth."[10] Surely it is true that Wescott, merely twenty years old at the time and midway through his "tortured young artist" phase, did load his verse with the more wearisome concerns of youth. Not all of his themes were insipid, though. One particularly relevant poem focused on the need to emancipate the human body from the chains of shame and guilt—an early, muted call for sexual freedom. The reality is that *The Bitterns* did possess literary merit, as well as furnishing a glimpse into the mind of an evolving writer and his heartfelt concerns as a young man. It also strengthened Wescott's confidence in his abilities as an artist and encouraged his pursuit of a literary career.

A year after the book's release, Wescott, now deeply committed to the art of writing, and Wheeler, equally intent on publishing, decided to broaden their knowledge by traveling to Europe to meet some of the continent's more illustrious wordsmiths. They succeeded in their aim, securing introductions to a host of literary figures, among them the novelist Ford Madox Ford. Despite being on a shoestring budget, they also managed to take in many sights during their stay, witnessing the grandeur of England and the destitution of postwar Germany, and forming memories that would linger and haunt them long after they had sailed back to the United States. Their impressions would eventually prompt them to relocate to Europe.

At this early date, however, Wescott and Wheeler could ill afford such an extravagance. Instead, the couple took an apartment in Manhattan, where Wheeler set to work acquiring additional funds for his publishing projects. Wescott, meanwhile, composed a series of poems, a collection released under the title, *Natives of Rock: XX Poems: 1921-1922*. Yet despite his burgeoning success as a poet, he was not satisfied with the direction his career was taking. He believed that he should be writing short stories and novels, not just poems, and so he began work on a piece of long fiction, an endeavor that culminated in the 1924 publication of his first novel, *The Apple of the Eye*.

Well-received by critics and public alike, the book centered on life in rural Wisconsin, a topic that showed up again and again in Wescott's early writings. The thrust of the story, according to one reviewer, was to prompt its young narrator "to break away from the puritanical inhibitions and harsh codes that weigh so heavily on the people of the region in order to seek a different destiny."[11] Certainly this was a subject close to its author's heart, since Wescott himself longed for a different destiny, even a different nation by this point. He had become amenable to the idea of returning to Europe to live and work, his opinion of life in the United States being one of palpable disdain. It was such condescension that infused an essay he wrote for the *Transatlantic Review* at this time, a piece ridiculing "the hypocrisy and vulgarity of American life," in the words of Noel Riley Fitch.[12] So it was that Wescott and Wheeler moved to France in 1925, where they remained for the next eight years. Like many expatriates, they considered it a magical nation, the fountainhead of modern culture, and therefore the place to be.

FRANCE IN THE JAZZ AGE

Scores of creative men and women flocked to Paris in the 1920s, attracted to the city's rich history, refined society, and romantic ambience. Artists were drawn to its resplendent architecture and to the soft, diffuse light that illuminated its streets, while dancers, from Isadora Duncan to Josephine Baker, reveled in its open-minded, high-spirited attitude. Writers were perhaps the most entranced by the city, with the *Dictionary of Literary Biography* listing nearly a hundred American authors who moved to Paris during this period.[13] If other types of artists are taken into account—musicians, painters, sculptors, and the like—this figure nearly triples. To be sure, the City of Light, a gracious and generous host to its American residents, offered the ideal conditions for one of the most innovative and industrious literary colonies in the Western world.

A large share of the writers hailed from the Midwest, so Wescott, had he desired it, would have been in familiar company. Although he and Wheeler took an apartment in the city's literary district, Wescott seldom socialized with his American colleagues, instead preferring to hobnob with British and French writers. He even affected a slight English accent at this time, prompting some of the Americans to dismiss him as shallow and pretentious. Such criticism notwithstanding, he did continue producing sophisticated literary works that impressed most readers but failed to move a smaller number who considered his style too mannered and self-conscious. One fault-finder was fellow expatriate Ernest Hemingway, who disliked both Wescott and his writings, and who did not hesitate to make his feelings known.

"Every word was written with the intention of making Glenway Wescott immortal," Hemingway complained to a journalist about one of Wescott's novels, a book that was published to glowing reviews.[14] Hemingway's disdain was not limited to his harsh comments to the press, however. He also put it into print, mocking Wescott by using him as the basis for a minor character in the novel, *The Sun Also Rises*. The fictional individual, an up-and-coming young novelist from Chicago who is living in Europe, is derided for being gay and speaking in a contrived fashion. "I just thought perhaps I was going to throw up," says the narrator upon meeting him.[15] Although Hemingway originally named the gay man Prescott, to rhyme with Wescott, his editor wisely persuaded him to change it. The contemptuous remarks, however, remained in place.

As for the reasons behind such hostility, Hemingway was a man who was prone to depression and who was troubled sexually as well, facts that became widely known and discussed after his suicide. It may have been the case, then, that his antigay posture grew out of his own sexual tensions and uncertainties.

It is also true that he was often jealous of other writers, particularly those who were more successful than he. The acclaim afforded Wescott in the late-1920s briefly overshadowed that of Hemingway, who did not attain his full measure of celebrity until the following decade. It is worth noting, too, that Hemingway's mother adored Wescott's work, even to the point of advising her son to use it as a model for his own writing, a recommendation that no doubt irked him. Then again, Hemingway's animosity may have been fueled by his conversations with his friend, the writer Gertrude Stein, who had a strong influence on the brusque author and who was herself less than complimentary when it came to Wescott.

A bold, imposing woman, Stein and her brother made their way to Paris in the early twentieth century, where they began collecting paintings by Cézanne, Gauguin, and Renoir. Stein also began collecting artists themselves, most notably Picasso and Matisse, as well as gifted young writers, all of whom frequented her apartment at 27 rue de Fleurus on the Left Bank. Soon, her salon became renowned for the brilliant visitors who passed through its doors, with Stein regarding herself as first among her peers. Indeed, this was a woman who once told Ezra Pound that she was one of three great Jewish geniuses, the others being Christ and Spinoza.[16] She summed up Wescott's work by saying, "he has a certain syrup but it does not pour," a judgment that was likely colored by her disapproval of his sexual orientation.[17] Stein, a lesbian, was as ignorant about gay male sexuality as was Hemingway himself.

"The act male homosexuals commit is ugly and repulsive and afterward they are disgusted with themselves," she once told Hemingway.

> They drink and take drugs, to palliate this, but they are disgusted with the act and they are always changing partners and cannot really be happy. In women it is the opposite. They do nothing that they are disgusted by and nothing that is repulsive and afterwards they are happy and they can lead happy lives together.[18]

So much for progressive thinking on the rue de Fleurus. Fortunately, a large share of expatriate writers were more knowledgeable about gay male sexuality, or at least more broad-minded, as well as appreciative of Wescott's considerable talents as an author. This was particularly the case after the release of *The Grandmothers,* his literary tour de force.

The Grandmothers

Wescott began writing his award-winning second novel soon after arriving in Paris and continued working on it when he and Wheeler moved, a few months later, to Villefranche-sur-Mer, a picturesque fishing village situated on the French Riviera near Nice. It was here that the couple, who had found themselves distracted by Parisian life, decided to settle in the hope that its bucolic conditions would prove more conducive to writing. Their intuition was right, with Wescott finishing his book at their hillside villa the following year.

Initially, he envisioned the work as an authentic history of his ancestors' lives in Wisconsin, but as the story unfolded he found it necessary to move into the realm of fiction, otherwise the book's scope would have been too limited. Comprised of fifteen chapters, twelve of which recount tales of Wescott's family in the 1800s, the story is told through a narrator, Alwyn Tower, an expatriate in Europe and Wescott's alter ego. In several respects, the novel is unconventional, including its incisive approach to the past.

"*The Grandmothers* is not simply another of those regional novels lauding the strength, endurance, foolhardiness and cleverness of the pioneers and sentimentalizing their dull lives," writes Ira Johnson.

> It is a rejection of the geographical frontier for a "migration to the frontier of imagination," increasing the spiritual territory of the American artist. Through him America may come to a similar self-awareness. The novel ceases to be a regional work and becomes one of the reality and myth of the American past.[19]

In the book, Alwyn Tower, the narrator, does not sanitize the historical figures in his family. Instead, he takes an unflinching look at both the weaknesses and the strengths of his Wisconsin ancestors, evaluating their moral worth while infusing his appraisal with a measured compassion.

He writes,

> Avid company of failures, out of date, behind the times, perhaps timeless. Ethically, socially, above all financially, they had made little progress; in modern methods of pretending to be happy, of pretending to have satisfied on earth their hearts' desires, they had made none at all. Pioneers because their unhappy dispositions unfitted them for everything else. . . . Imaginative but disillusioned; therefore talented for the sake of God, religious in hope of heaven.[20]

From such passages, it is evident that Tower's view of his ancestors is harsh in certain respects, but elsewhere in the novel it is respectful, even sympathetic. By the end of the story, he has gained a better understanding of these imperfect individuals and, along with this knowledge, a better chance of letting go of his family's past as he moves toward his own future.

Surprisingly, given its nonsentimental approach to the American experience, the novel was a resounding success when it was released in 1927, winning the esteemed Harper Prize Novel Award. In its first six months, it enjoyed twenty-six printings and established Wescott as one of the most accomplished writers of his generation. He did not rest on his laurels, however, but instead prepared for the release of *Good-Bye Wisconsin,* his next book.

Good-Bye Wisconsin

Published in 1928, *Good-Bye Wisconsin* is composed of the title essay and ten short stories, and, like *The Grandmothers,* is narrated by Alwyn Tower, who travels from his home in Europe to his family's farm in the Midwest for an extended stay. With this set-up in place, Wescott is in a position to express his opinion on an array of topics about contemporary life. The narrator finds fault with much of American society, and perhaps this is why it comes as no surprise when, at the end of the book, he is glad to wrap up his visit and sail back to Europe. The book's title implies a "letting go" of an attachment to Wisconsin, but Wescott does not actually say farewell. He does distance himself from his origins, however, by revealing his distaste for certain aspects of life in the Midwest and for life in America itself.

Wescott placed the short story "Adolescence" in the collection, the one in which he modeled the two principal characters after himself and his first boyfriend. In it, the Wescott character, an "effeminate, rustic boy," attends, with his fifteen-year-old male friend, a costume party dressed as a girl.[21] In the course of the evening, another boy, believing the Wescott character to be female, tries to kiss him, a turn of events that both alarms and confuses the young protagonist. Among other things, the author's intention was to illustrate the perplexing emotions experienced by the gay youth who is becoming aware of his sexuality.

In another tale, "The Sailor," a young man from rural Wisconsin joins the military and finds himself shipped off to Villefranche. Once there, he falls hard for a prostitute name Zizi, who before long takes on a lesbian lover. To resolve this thorny complication, the three form a triangular relationship which eventually proves unfulfilling, even humiliating, to the American. Even so, when he returns to the family farm in Wisconsin, he finds himself yearning for life abroad. The sailor, writes Wescott, had become "lonesome for temptation and regret, for sharp contrasts, for distinct good and evil—in other words, for Europe—but at the same time he hated these things from the bottom of his heart because they had made a fool of him."[22]

At this juncture, one might ask why Wescott, who was living comfortably in the south of France, would persist in writing about the United States, a nation from which he had tried to escape. The most probable explanation is that he had never made peace with his background, that he was still confronting his thoughts and feelings in print. Surely it is true, as critic William Rueckert has pointed out, that "Wescott's imaginative and creative life was lived in Wisconsin,"[23] even as he toiled in France, a sentiment echoed in the following entry in the 1940 compendium *Contemporary American Authors:*

> [Wescott] finds it impossible to break away from his middle western background, dreadful as he thinks it, and, although unable to accept Wisconsin, he cannot escape it. He feels that literary treatment of Americans, whom he professes to like until they reach about the senior year of college, must be analytical and diagnostic.[24]

Still, it is important to note that Wescott was not alone in his fixation with his homeland or in his critical stance toward it. Many expatriates in France wrote about the United States, a stock explanation being that the distance between the two nations offered an enhanced perspective, a greater clarity, about life in America. In this, there is no doubt a degree of truth.

Life in Villefranche was golden. Wescott adored France even as he wrote about the United States, his European years being among his happiest and most productive. When he was not writing, he and Wheeler socialized with the other writers and artists who lived in the village, with Wescott developing a particular fondness for Isadora Duncan whose memoir he was proofreading at the time of her bizarre death. He also struck up a lasting friendship with Jean Cocteau, who was living with a young man in a quaint Villefranche hotel. Before long, Wescott would himself take a lover, Jacques Guérin, whom he met on a trip to Paris.

The son of a wealthy perfume manufacturer and department store magnate, Guérin was stately, smart, and sexy. Powerfully drawn to him, Wescott befriended the genteel young man and their attachment soon blossomed into a romance that endured for years. In reality, it would be the first of many such affairs Wescott would enjoy in his lifetime, with Wheeler likewise plunging into extracurricular intimacies on a regular basis. The one lover both of them would share, however, entered their lives during a brief stay in New York City during the winter of 1926, when Wescott delivered the manuscript of *The Grandmothers* to his publisher.

His name was George Platt Lynes and he was a charmer. While still in his teens, he had toured Europe, and, with a friend, published a series of chapbooks. Then, at the age of twenty, he had opened a bookshop in New Jersey and it was at this time that the couple met him. By all accounts, the willowy young man made quite an impression on the two men, Wescott in particular.

When the couple returned to their home in Villefranche a few weeks later, Wescott initiated a correspondence with Lynes, impassioned letters that continued for a year and a half until, at last, Lynes moved to France and into the couple's villa. There he lived for several months at a time, during which he made love to both Wescott and Wheeler, although he was more attracted to the latter. All the same, they were a trio and made no effort to conceal the fact, ultimately becoming one of the most famous gay threesomes of the era. Furthermore, they remained attached for the next quarter of a century despite the fact that they did not always live together. This was particularly the case after Lynes, who embarked on a photography career shortly after moving in with the couple, began attracting international attention for his work. As could be expected, his growing fame brought with it the need for frequent travel. As for Wescott, he not only remained tied to Wheeler and Lynes during this period, the late 1920s and early 1930s, but also continued romancing Guérin, visiting the young aristocrat on business trips to Paris. Most often, these excursions centered on Wheeler's burgeoning career as a publisher. Certainly it was an opportune time and place in which to pursue such a vocation.

Harrison of Paris

In Paris during the Jazz Age, numerous small presses began springing up, many of which became renowned for producing high-quality books and prints. One such enterprise was established by American expatriate Barbara Harrison, a sunny, carefree, and astute young heiress from California who adored literature and wished to involve herself meaningfully in the Parisian literary community. Since Harrison was also a close friend of Wescott and Wheeler, she appealed to these trusted companions to join her, and they readily agreed. With Harrison supplying the capital, Wheeler assuming the role of director, and Wescott serving as translator and advisor, Harrison of Paris was inaugurated in 1930. In October of that year the company published its first book, a re-issue of Shakespeare's *Venus and Adonis,* presented with elegance and distinction.

During the next four years, Harrison of Paris produced a dozen more books, all of them artfully crafted with the highest standards in mind. Among the authors whose work it re-issued were Thomas Mann, Lord Byron, Bret Harte, and Fyodor Dostoyevski. The company also published a French songbook, the contents of which were selected by Katherine Anne Porter, another Wescott friend and the author of *Ship of Fools.* Harrison of Paris published two new works by Wescott himself, most notably *The Babe's Bed,* his final Wisconsin story.

The Babe's Bed

A thirty-five-page allegory, *The Babe's Bed* makes use of a narrator, but this time it is an anonymous storyteller rather than Alwyn Tower. The story is different in another respect as well. Midway through the tale of a Wisconsin farm family, the narrator undergoes an inner crisis. He realizes that the story he is telling is merely an amalgam of his perceptions, memories, and interpretations of events rather than an actual depiction of the events themselves, that he cannot escape the element of subjectivity when attempting to objectively describe and attribute meaning to an external occurrence. This means, then, that the tale he has begun to spin is merely an aberration, a fantasy. In this book and in this unorthodox manner Wescott subverts the narrative process itself and finally says good-bye to his Wisconsin roots, as well as bidding farewell more generally to his quest for truth as a Jazz Age fiction writer. It has been noted that he ends *The Babe's Bed* with the word "asleep," and this is entirely appropriate in that he would not write another novel for a decade.

Although the print run of *The Babe's Bed* was just under 400 copies, due to Wescott's sterling reputation the story was reviewed by several prominent newspapers, including *The New York Times.* Although most of the reviews were respectful, they noted that the author appeared to be faltering, that the promise he had previously shown seemed to be reaching its peak prematurely. As time would reveal, the critics were wrong; his best work was yet to come. That said, it is true that Wescott did lack inspiration at this juncture. No longer motivated to devise fictional accounts of life in the Midwest, he had become an author without a topic. There is also reason to believe that he was curious to try his hand at nonfiction writing but was unable to find compelling subject matter. Consequently, he turned his attention to other aspects of literary life as he waited for his muse to return.

During this period he devoted his efforts to helping Barbara Harrison and Monroe Wheeler develop the publishing company. More and more, he and Wheeler spent their days not at their villa in the South of France but in Paris, where they lived in a posh apartment owned by Harrison and situated on the Left Bank. George Platt Lynes leased a nearby flat. In the city, Wescott passed his days translating classical literature and performing other tasks on behalf of the company, then used his evenings to entertain potential business associates. In his spare time, he fraternized with British and French writers as he had done in the past when he lived in Paris, while continuing to keep his distance from the American authors in residence. "Hemingway despised me, Fitzgerald was a drinker with a miserable wife, and the Americans who hung around the cafés bored me to death," he said.[25]

Fear and Trembling

One matter that did not bore Wescott was the gathering storm in Germany. During the late summer months of 1931, he toured the volatile country with Wheeler, Lynes, Harrison, and a chauffeur. The nation's tense political atmosphere captured the author's attention and inspired him as a writer. This was a time when Hitler's *Mein Kampf* was a bestseller, and the Nazi Party was the second largest political bloc in the nation. Disturbed by the rampant unemployment and frenzied nationalism he observed, as well as by the impending violence he sensed, Wescott felt obliged to warn the American people of what would culminate in the ascension of the Third Reich later in the decade. With this aim in mind, he set to work writing several essays upon returning to France, which he completed the following spring and collectively titled *Fear and Trembling*. A 370-page tome, he dedicated the book to his traveling companions: "For B. H. and M. W. and G. P. L., this troubled record and unexpected result of our trip to

Germany in August and September, 1931, with love and various thanks."[26] He then dispatched the dense manuscript to his publisher in New York with a message of urgency. Sensitive to his concerns, Harper and Brothers released the book with a modicum of editing merely two months after receiving it—and to a wholly unforeseen reaction. *Fear and Trembling* simply annoyed the critics and left the reading public unmoved.

The problem was that Wescott was neither a political scientist nor a historian. He was a thirty-one-year-old poet and fiction writer whose attempt to analyze the complex conditions of prewar Europe and to prescribe various treatments, were, in the words of one modern critic, "naïve and facile, redundant and self-contradictory."[27] Not surprisingly, the book damaged Wescott's reputation and undermined his self-confidence. His political writings were not only rejected, however, they were also ridiculed in certain quarters. His antagonist Ernest Hemingway used the occasion to sneer at the author's efforts to mobilize the citizenry.

"Glenway Wescott, this is no kidding, is issuing a Call to Arms," Hemingway wrote to fellow author John Dos Passos when he heard about the book. "He feels things are in A BAD WAY."[28]

In fact, things were in a bad way and much of the world already sensed it, but this did not absolve Wescott's hurriedly concocted essays. His knee-jerk response to failure worsened matters. It appears that he tried to divert public attention from the muddle by publishing his next book as quickly as possible. In this way *A Calendar of Saints for Unbelievers* came into existence, a work released by Harrison of Paris that same year and intended as a whimsical look at the Christian saints. In reality, the book, which has been described as "undisciplined and self-indulgent," succeeded only in fueling speculation that Wescott was a writer suffering from a paucity of ideas, an artist squandering his talent.[29]

Disappointed with the downward turn his career had taken and no longer smitten with his part-time lover Jacques Guérin, Wescott decided to make sweeping changes in his life, first and foremost by returning to the United States to live and work. He asked Wheeler and Lynes to accompany him, but Wheeler was hesitant for business reasons. Immersed in his job overseeing Harrison of Paris, he feared that leaving France would spell the end of the publishing company, a worry that ultimately proved justified. Lynes, on the other hand, readily agreed, particularly since he was already spending substantial amounts of time in New York City on photography assignments. He even kept an apartment there. Furthermore, Barbara Harrison also was willing to return, as she was worried about the prospects of war in Europe. Wheeler bowed to his friends' pressure and finally yielded. The four expatriates moved to Manhattan in 1934, at a time when the city was still reeling from the devastating effects of the Great Depression and when gay men and lesbians, after a respite during the Jazz Age, were once again feeling the lash of discrimination.

THE MANHATTAN YEARS

When Wescott and his party returned to the United States, the economic situation was bleak. In the early 1930s, thirteen million people had suddenly been thrown out of work, a million of whom lived in New York City. There, a hundred thousand residents had been evicted from their homes and forced to find lodging in shelters, parks, and abandoned buildings. Some lived on the streets or in alleyways, while a smaller number sought refuge inside the city's huge water mains. Many of these people had been executives, teachers, nurses, shop-keepers, and artists before the Great Depression. No profession was spared.

Fortunately, matters began to improve in 1934 when Fiorello La Guardia was installed as mayor of New York City. Although the measures he put into place were more or less successful in helping the city get back on its feet, the stalwart politician was not without his faults.

A judgmental autocrat with a short fuse, La Guardia was known for alienating minority groups during his tenure in office, groups that included the homosexual citizenry. He permitted, even encouraged, his underlings to entrap and prosecute gay men and lesbians, thus perpetuating an ugly state of affairs that had begun during the previous administration against a segment of the population that, during the Jazz Age, the city had otherwise accepted.

Gays and lesbians in Manhattan during the 1920s had lived fairly open lives, mingling freely and comfortably with heterosexuals in much the same way that Wescott, Wheeler, and Lynes had done in Paris. The situation had deteriorated when the stock market crashed. Of the countless citizens thrown out of work, most were men, many

of whom found their identities as males ruptured. They felt emascu-
lated because their roles as their families' breadwinners had been
stripped away. Unfortunately, one consequence of this epidemic of
male insecurity was an abrupt return to traditional and prejudicial no-
tions of gender, including renewed homophobia typified by police
crackdowns on the gay citizenry.

Arriving in the city during this troubling time, Wescott and his
partners were witnesses to this legally sanctioned oppression that
Wescott, in particular, found deeply disturbing. The three men could
nevertheless count themselves among the lucky ones. Not all gay
New Yorkers were equally vulnerable when it came to police harassment. Those who were socially or politically prominent were far less
likely to suffer persecution at the hands of the authorities. Wescott,
Wheeler, and Lynes discovered that the public held them in rather
high esteem, thus their reputations helped shield them from mistreat-
ment.

The three men leased a spacious apartment in Manhattan, with
Wescott taking one bedroom and Wheeler and Lynes sharing a bedroom of their own. They agreed on this arrangement because Wheeler
and Lynes were the more sexually involved of the trio. Wescott had
stopped having sex with Wheeler by the time they moved back to the
United States. Their continued attachment was based instead on a
shared history, mutual affection, and intellectual compatibility.

Wescott and his partners were able to enjoy substantial freedom of
movement in their social lives in Manhattan's antigay milieu. As priv-
ileged gay men, they could congregate in glitzy nightclubs, the kind
of high-toned establishments the police rarely raided. They could
also gather at private parties or at performances of the Metropolitan
Opera, the Met being "standard meeting place" for gay men, according to one source from the era.[30] Such liberty allowed Wescott and his
partners to become better acquainted with other influential gay men
and lesbians in Manhattan, and also permitted them to become more
widely known themselves. Their prominence steadily rose and the
three soon became the toast of the town, with little need to worry
about the prying eyes of the vice squad or the wagging tongues of the
gossip columnists.

Regarding their careers, Lynes was fast becoming the most acclaimed, his photographs winning praise from American and European art critics, as well as from Hollywood movie moguls who soon

began commissioning him to photograph some of the era's most glamorous film stars. He also performed assignments for several high-profile magazines and upscale stores, among them *Vogue, Harper's Bazaar,* Saks Fifth Avenue, and Bergdorf Goodman. In addition, he turned his lens toward an array of nude men, all of them sleek and beautiful. Among his subjects were a dancer from a famed Russian ballet troupe and a renowned African-American jazz singer from Harlem, both of whom also enjoyed sexual trysts with Glenway Wescott during this time. The black-and-white images that Lynes produced were invariably striking in composition and lighting, and proved to be very popular with private collectors.

Ironically, at the same time Lynes' career was accelerating, that of Monroe Wheeler was grinding to a halt. A year after moving to Manhattan, he had no choice but to close Harrison of Paris, which had set up shop in the United States. As with other small publishing companies during the Depression years, it simply could not stay afloat financially while retaining its commitment to quality book production. Wheeler did not remain jobless for long, thanks to his connections in Manhattan's gay world, especially with Lynes.

Wheeler wished to join the staff of an art museum and his relationship with the photographer proved invaluable. Lynes introduced him to Lincoln Kirstein, one of the century's most important patrons of the arts and a figure well placed in New York City's artistic, literary, and gay communities. The son of a department store magnate, Kirstein, while a student at Harvard, had established the literary quarterly *Hound & Horn,* which published the works of such up-and-coming poets as e. e. cummings, Ezra Pound, and T. S. Eliot. He also convinced Russian choreographer George Balanchine to immigrate to the United States, where together they formed what would become the New York City Ballet. As well, he helped establish the Harvard Society for Contemporary Art, which evolved into the Museum of Modern Art (MoMA). It was at MoMA that Wheeler's connections landed him a job as a catalog designer, although he soon began playing a far more vital role, that of a liaison between the museum and the innovative French painters he had befriended during his expatriate years.

As for Wescott's career, he was blocked as a writer. Twice during the 1930s he began working on novels but was unable to finish them despite the encouragement of friends and relatives. In reality, their well-intentioned prodding may have been part of the problem.

Wescott's instincts as an author did not lie in novels. He was, at his best, an essayist and a short story writer, as he eventually realized. Even his finest fictional work, *The Pilgrim Hawk,* which was still to come, is typically described as a "short novel," with some categorizing it a novella. Regardless, those in his circle pressed him to write full-length novels because they considered such works to be the most prestigious of his literary repertoire, as well as the ones that generated the most income. When the author found it impossible to comply, he became disappointed in himself, partly because he felt beholden to his loved ones who so often supported him financially so he could devote his days to writing.

Adding to the pressure, Wescott was expected to be not only a novelist, but a world class, award-winning one, which was problematical because he had never possessed a great deal of confidence in his abilities even under the best of circumstances. Furthermore, the trouncing he had endured for his most recent books, *Calendar of the Saints* and *Fear and Trembling,* had further eroded what remained of his self-assurance. He thus found himself in the unenviable position of being expected to produce magnificent works of fiction while suffering serious doubts about his literary prowess.

Then, too, he lacked inspiration. Certainly it is true that once Wescott came to terms with his bitter feelings about his past in the Midwest, his imagination seemed to dry up, at least for a time. "What was left for him to write about?" asked Bruce Bawer in a 1988 essay about the author. "Wescott could hardly write about the life he was leading with Monroe Wheeler."[31]

Stalled by a dearth of ideas, Wescott immersed himself in the excitement of Manhattan as he had done in Paris when he had suffered creative droughts. This was easy for him to do, since Manhattan's social scene was a high-spirited one and thus served as an effective distraction. But Bawer may have been onto something when he alluded to Wescott's inability to chronicle his life with Wheeler. It is altogether possible that Wescott did have meaningful ideas for fiction—ideas that grew out of his experiences as a gay man—but was aware that such subject matter could, and undoubtedly would, create formidable difficulties for him both personally and professionally.

Gay Literature in the 1930s

In Europe and the United States during the Depression era there were several renowned novelists who were gay or lesbian, but none of them published books having gay themes. Society would not countenance it. Only a few years earlier, in 1928, the English writer Radclyffe Hall released her prim novel of lesbian love, *The Well of Loneliness,* and found herself rebuked by the courts, a state of affairs that paralyzed other authors who wished to write about same-sex issues. This does not mean that gay writers did not write stories and books containing homosexual content. Some did, but they did not endeavor to publish them.

E. M. Forster, for instance, one of Wescott's friends, wrote the gay-themed *Maurice,* a manuscript that Wescott read and determined to see in print someday. He and Christopher Isherwood suggested to Forster that he allow it to be published after his death, and the author agreed. Even so, it was still uncertain whether the book would ever see the light of day. On this subject, Forster, an early advocate of gay equality, was perhaps less optimistic than Wescott about future generations' attitudes toward homosexuality. It has even been suggested that Forster's doubts may have spurred him to stop writing novels altogether at the age of forty-five, after the publication of *A Passage to India.* "The discovery of a romantic happiness that could not, in Forster's lights, be portrayed in fiction helped to turn him away from the novel," says Margot Livesey.[32]

Wescott composed a graphic and rather lengthy gay love story in 1938 titled "A Visit to Priapus." The tale recounts a weekend of same-sex lovemaking between narrator Alwyn Tower and a young painter from Maine who lacks social polish but sports an impressive endowment. It was based on a real-life experience in which Wescott, sexually desperate, traveled to Maine for a pre-arranged rendezvous with just such a man. Although the resultant story was not published while Wescott was still alive—it would be nearly sixty years before it appeared in print—it nevertheless confirms that he did have an interest in writing gay fiction. His limited output during the 1930s may have been related to an unwillingness on the part of English-language publishers to release literary works having same-sex themes.

Of course, a secondary reason may have been related to Wescott's loved ones. It seems that those closest to him were unwilling to sanction gay content in his work, with his brother and sister-in-law, as well as his partner, actively discouraging him from writing about same-sex relations. In a 1956 journal entry, the author refers to their position on the subject, then alludes to his own trepidation: "My feeling of being prevented from writing about homosexuality (by Monroe + Lloyd + Barbara) equals in an important degree my own inhibition," he notes.[33] But as "A Visit to Priapus" reveals, such impediments did not stop him from exploring same-sex themes entirely.

As a story based on true events, the tale, particularly its central section, reveals a great deal about Wescott as a person and a sexual being. Written in his characteristically stately style, "A Visit to Priapus" is marked by his penchant for icy analyses of flawed human figures. It is surely no exaggeration to say that the story's narrator, essentially Wescott himself, looks down on the somewhat provincial painter with whom he has sex. After spending the night with the artist, the narrator dissects the young man emotionally, as insecure people are occasionally wont to do. At the same time, though, the narrator also demeans himself. Because the painter, dubbed the "Maine Priapus," appears to be less than fully aroused by their lovemaking, the narrator assumes it is because he himself is unappealing. "I am not an Adonis," he says.

> Maine Priapus simply may not have found me exciting. None of those I have gone to bed with just lately has. Only half a dozen all my life have—and then not really until I had a chance to deploy other aspects of myself than my sketchy, faulty physique . . .[34]

The storyteller does not stop there, however. He projects his own emotions and aspirations onto his hapless lover, even to the point of suggesting that the painter may have had an ulterior motive for agreeing to their encounter in the first place, with such distrust further betraying the author's insecurity. Specifically, he believes the painter's participation may have been merely a self-serving scheme. "The mediocrity of his pleasure did not matter to him because he had an eye on a more important advantage," says the narrator, concluding that it is his own fame the Maine Priapus hoped to exploit. "I personified the world: society and celebrity and luxury."[35]

It is telling, of course, that the narrator would interpret the awkward actions of an inexperienced and possibly intimidated young lover as calculating, since Wescott himself characteristically sought out the rich and famous who often proved useful to him, financially as well as socially. It is surely no stretch to propose that he may have been seeing his own ambition in the artist. Whether or not this was the case, one thing is evident: Wescott, to protect himself emotionally, seems to have felt the need to keep a distance between himself and those with whom he had sex, the predictable result of serious self-doubt.

Also, Wescott's literary reputation was less than gratifying at this time mainly because he was not publishing books. Yet even if he had been releasing such works, his image might still have been less than stellar, since many readers had begun to consider him passé, along with Gertrude Stein and certain other Jazz Age writers. In their opinion, his mannered style of writing and conspicuous class consciousness no longer had a place in American literature, the Great Depression having so totally altered society that his prose had become irrelevant.

Fortunately, one area in which Wescott did excel in the 1930s involved public speaking on literary topics. With his resonant voice, refined diction, and impressive knowledge of literature, he quickly became a respected and popular lecturer. He also renewed his interest in the art world at this point and published several accomplished essays on aspects of the visual arts. Despite the favorable reception his talks and essays received, his loved ones continued pressing him to write another novel.

Seeking inspiration for such a book, Wescott returned to France for a visit, where he reunited with old friends and old flames, among them Jacques Guérin. Although the excursion provided an enjoyable change of scenery, it did not offer up the inspiration he sought. What did stimulate him was a journal he began keeping around this time. Indeed, recording his experiences proved so meaningful to Wescott that he soon began encouraging his colleagues to do the same. Besides helping him recall and organize, on paper, important moments in his life, his memoirs proved indispensable in helping modern readers understand his inner world after his demise.

Another means by which Wescott sought to jump-start his creativity was by reducing the distractions of Manhattan. This he accomplished by spending time at a New Jersey farm, one reminiscent of his boyhood home. Owned by his younger brother Lloyd and his brother's

new wife, Barbara Harrison, he savored the peace of mind the pasto-
ral setting offered him.

Lloyd and Barbara had met in Manhattan the previous year, where
Lloyd held a job at Harper and Brothers. Like Glenway, he too had
left Wisconsin far behind. Upon being introduced, the couple hit it off
immediately and married within the year. It was in this way that
Barbara Harrison, the heiress, became Glenway's sister-in-law and
Wheeler and Lynes's lifelong friend. Lloyd had long dreamed of becoming a gentleman farmer and with his new wife's fortune was able
to bring his fantasy to fruition. The couple purchased a sprawling estate near the town of Hampton in the northwestern part of the state,
with their escape to the country reflecting the growing trend among
moneyed Manhattanites to exchange the surging metropolis for the
comparative tranquility of rural living.

It was precisely such serenity that Glenway Wescott needed, and
found, on the farm. Each weekend, he, Wheeler, and Lynes headed
for the estate, where they took one of the property's farmhand dwell-
ings as their own, renovated it, and christened it "Stone-blossom." It
became their hideaway, their sanctuary, and, for Wescott, the place
that most inspired him to compose poetry and, more important, to begin work on *The Pilgrim Hawk*. This would be his one true master-
piece, a work of intelligence and eloquence.

The Pilgrim Hawk

Set in a graceful country house in the French village of Chancellet,
The Pilgrim Hawk's central players consist of Alexandra Henry, a
wealthy American expatriate who owns the estate, and narrator Alwyn
Tower, her guest. Two servants are also present in the house, an amorous Moroccan couple named Jean and Eve.

Into this peaceful domestic scene comes an Irish couple, Larry and
Madeleine Cullen, their chauffeur Ricketts, and Madeleine's pet
hawk Lucy, which she keeps tethered to her arm. This unlikely assortment of personalities, en route to Budapest for a holiday, pauses at the
country house for an afternoon visit with the Americans.

As the tale unfolds, readers learn that Larry is an alcoholic who
Madeleine attempts to keep sober by engaging in diversions such as
traveling, hunting, and Irish politics. Not surprisingly, their marriage
is not a happy one; it is an exercise in emotional and spiritual suffoca-

tion. Larry detests the hawk, convinced that Madeleine is using it to keep his romantic attentions at bay. He may be right, moreover, since the bird attacks him whenever he tries to touch his wife. At the same time, Larry identifies with the captive pet, in that he feels his wife is keeping him tethered to their marriage.

As could be expected, the Cullen's difficulties quickly come to the surface, with the narrator observing and mentally passing judgment on their marred union throughout the remainder of the story. Describing the couple as "self-centered without any introspection, strenuous but emotionally idle,"[36] he dismisses them as "coldly gregarious, mere passers of time."[37] In due course, he does develop a degree of compassion for them, however, and especially for their enslaved pet.

At the same time the Cullens are exposing their marital flaws in the great room and the garden, another tense situation is brewing in the kitchen. Ricketts, the chauffeur, is showing undue attention to Eve, thereby causing Jean to become jealous. Soon, this erupts into a dispute, one that corresponds to the more consequential clash taking place at the same moment involving the Cullens and their hawk. The upshot is that the embarrassed couple, their pet, and their driver abruptly leave Chancellet, thus bringing to a close their strained visit.

This is not the end of the tale, however. After their departure, the narrator talks to his host about the odd visitors and gains crucial information about their histories, facts that cause him to realize that his earlier conclusions about them had been wrong. He therefore begins to doubt his own perceptions, this being the same process that occurred in *The Babe's Bed* when the narrator came to question his own experience of reality.

"Half the time, I am afraid, my opinion of people is just guessing; cartooning," says the narrator after the Cullen's departure.

> Again and again, I give way to a kind of inexact and vengeful lyricism, and I am ashamed of it. Sometimes I doubt entirely my judgment in moral matters; and so long as I propose to be a story-teller, that is the whisper of the devil for me.[38]

At one point, the narrator criticizes his literary abilities even more direly, declaring, in essence, that he is unfit to be a writer. "No one warned me that I really did not have talent enough," he says.[39] Of course, his low opinion of his abilities mirrors Wescott's longstanding insecurities as an author. But as it turns out, he had no reason to judge himself so harshly, as *The Pilgrim Hawk* would reveal. The book immediately re-established him as one of the most inventive writers of the era, and rightfully so.

Among the novel's admirable qualities is its structure, which is complex and sophisticated. Set in 1939, the narrator recalls his experiences in France during the 1920s, an arrangement that allows him to reflect upon his earlier reflections. Time is thus placed within itself.

Wescott also arranged it so that the plot of the novel, while moving forward in a conventional linear sequence, permits the storyteller to use its events as a springboard for inner musings on associated matters. In this way, the narrator's mental processes juxtapose other times, places, and events onto the main story line, which continues progressing at a steady pace.

Another unique aspect of *The Pilgrim Hawk* involves the storyteller's perspective, which is the reverse of that found in Wescott's earlier works. This time, the tale is told by an American citizen living in the United States who recounts his past as an expatriate in France. Wescott further uses the book to scrutinize members of the upper class, whereas his previous works targeted those of the middle and lower classes, most notably the rural poor.

Wescott focuses on the triangularity of the toxic relationships depicted in the novel. As we have seen, Wescott had a lifelong penchant for threesomes, his ménage à trois with Wheeler and Lynes being but one manifestation. In *The Pilgrim Hawk,* he creates the triad of Larry and Madeleine Cullen and their pet Lucy, as well as that of the servants Jean and Eve and the chauffeur Ricketts. These two trios clash within themselves while also paralleling and overlapping with one another.

Finally, in regard to symbolism, the author refuses to assign the title's hawk a static meaning but instead applies to it multiple representations depending on the context. The bird represents, alternatively, the aridity of bachelorhood, the power of erotic desire, the threat of impending death, and the acuteness of conscious awareness, with the shackled hawk symbolizing the imprisoned nature, the suppression of instinct. The author thus employs the animal in an innovative fashion, as a revolving symbol, ever changing and responsive to the needs of the story.

The tale itself became an American classic that has been anthologized repeatedly since its original publication, impacting Wescott's life by rekindling his faltering career and motivating him to persist as a writer.

He now spent increasing amounts of time engaged in writing at Stone-blossom, even moving full-time to the estate in 1943. As fate would have it, this was the same year that a part-time lover of Lynes was killed in the war, a loss that devastated the photographer. So shaken was Lynes that he left Wescott and Wheeler at Stone-blossom and took up with his deceased lover's brother. Not long afterward, Lynes moved to the West Coast to get on with his life, as well as to advance his photography career.

Wescott continued romancing attractive men on occasion, as did Wheeler, who by now had become a personage in the Manhattan art world. Not that Wescott was lacking in public acclaim. In the early to mid-1940s, he composed short stories, essays, and another novel, a literary resurrection that appears to have been stimulated in large part by international events.

"In many ways, it was really World War II which either shocked Wescott into writing fiction or acted upon him in some way to start him writing again," says William Rueckert. "Every one of the fictional or creative works which he produced from 1940 through 1944 is directly or indirectly related to the war, and one of them is actually a war novel."[40]

Wescott's short stories included "Mr. Auerbach in Paris," in which narrator Alwyn Tower recalls his visit with a benevolent German Jew in 1923. In the story, the Jewish gentleman, Auerbach, glimpses the splendor of Paris with his friend Tower and declares that the City of Light would be even finer if Germany possessed it. Auerbach obviously has enormous respect for his nation and its potential greatness. The narrator, in retrospect, is struck by the fact that Germans like Auerbach failed to foresee that their country, humiliated and debilitated by World War I, would eventually travel a malevolent course in a rabid quest for power and vengeance. They also could not have anticipated that it would turn against those having a Jewish heritage, even to the point of annihilating them.

A second story, "The Frenchman Six Feet Three," again uses a retrospective narrative with Alywn Tower in 1943, recalling events in France in 1938. The tale is essentially a lamentation, one that looks at France before and after the German invasion, with a focus on the unfortunate consequences of the military defeat. Critics have noted that

Wescott, in a departure from his usual approach, does not coldly analyze the characters in this story—the title's tall Frenchman stands as a
respectful symbol of the stature of France—but rather retains an element of humanity and a respect for the losses sustained by the French
people during the war. "(I)n the personal and cultural situation,"
writes Ira Johnson, "the sad, pitiful, and complex qualities are not ignored."[41]

Wescott's war novel, *Apartment in Athens,* was published in 1945,
and although it attracted favorable reviews and sold over a half-million copies during its first year in print, it proved to be the last one he
would ever write. The story takes place in Athens during the German
occupation of Greece, where Ernst Kalter, a captain in the German
military, moves into a four-room apartment in which a Greek family
still dwells. His unwelcome presence in their home symbolizes Germany's occupation of surrounding European nations. The hapless
family is composed of Nicholas, the mild-mannered father and part
owner of a small publishing business, his wife, and their young son
and daughter. The latter, who is ten years old, is mute after having
witnessed German soldiers slaughtering Greek citizens in the streets
of Athens.

The novel follows this assemblage of characters for several months,
in the course of which Nicholas attempts to appease the German captain but eventually is imprisoned and executed. Before his death,
however, he manages to smuggle an impassioned letter to his wife in
which he makes clear his belief that Germany, even if defeated in the
war, will rise again and wreak destruction on the world. Humankind
must therefore be vigilant, he insists.

"They will let us come up again for a season; then when the time is
ripe for them, mow all our lives down again in a disgusting, useless
harvest like this," he says of the Germans.[42] Nicholas then suggests a
recipe for lasting peace, one that is more political than philosophical,
namely, the intervention of the Americans. "(I) feel sure that they will
be most important again when the war is over," he says.

> Probably the Russians are ruthless, but the British have too
> much sense of honor and sentiment for the job that is to be done;
> and the Americans can influence the British. It is important for
> them to be told what we have learned from German rule and
> misrule.[43]

Inspired by the letter, the man's wife, now widowed, becomes involved in the fight against German tyranny, the son joins the Greek military, and the daughter, shocked by the execution, once again finds her voice. In effect, the father's murder serves as a catalyst, revitalizing the persecuted family and stirring it to action.

It is perhaps telling that in this novel Wescott views fascism in the same way that he viewed puritanism in his first novel, *The Apple of the Eye.* He regards both as killers of the soul, as afflictions capable of exterminating love and the sense of self, which is a viewpoint that may well have been related to his Midwestern upbringing. As a young gay man growing up in rural Wisconsin, he no doubt acutely experienced the region's heavy conservatism, including its strict sexual mores. Thus, the fact that his novels repeatedly explore the paralysis caused by social and political oppression may indicate just how strongly his childhood and adolescence affected him. Certainly his background would help explain why he felt compelled to live and work abroad for so many years.

Apartment in Athens, although applauded by the critics and embraced by the public, nevertheless contained weaknesses, most notably flaws in characterization and narrative voice. It is also generally conceded that Wescott was heavy-handed in presenting the story's moral truths about war. Apparently he felt such explicitness was warranted, and even used the novel to support American involvement in the war. On the back cover of the book's first edition is a statement by Wescott advocating war bonds, accompanied by a photograph of the author taken by George Platt Lynes. Wescott also embarked on a publicity tour on behalf of the war bond effort, along with several other writers. In this unabashedly patriotic fashion, he wrapped up his career as a novelist.

Although *Apartment in Athens* marked the end of his days as a creator of lengthy works of fiction, it did not signify the end of Wescott's writing career. He continued composing poetry, short stories, and essays in the ensuing years. He also continued displaying the activist tendencies he had begun to exhibit during wartime, leanings that would persist, strengthen, and eventually yield benefits for both the literary and gay communities.

THE ACTIVIST YEARS

At the end of World War II, Wescott decided to make the United States his permanent home. For income he wrote short pieces, including critical reviews, and lectured at colleges and universities across the nation, his discourses centering on the works of authors such as Ernest Hemingway, Thornton Wilder, Gertrude Stein, and Virginia Woolf. He also found himself being called upon, more and more, to serve as an elder statesman of American literature even though he was only in his middle years at this point.

In the late 1940s, for instance, he was appointed Chairman of the National Commission for UNESCO, a United Nations role that required him to grapple with censorship laws and related matters. He also became involved with the Authors Guild and PEN, a worldwide organization of poets, essayists, and novelists, and was elected by his peers to membership in the National Institute of Arts and Letters, a prestigious body to which he devoted enormous amounts of time and energy over the next two decades. Politically, Wescott used his influence to defend controversial figures such as Elizabeth Ames, a woman persecuted for her advocacy of writers during the McCarthy era.

Ames, an erudite and equitable woman, had been the executive director of the Yaddo Writers Colony in Saratoga Springs, New York, since 1923, where she welcomed all manner of authors to the spacious wooded estate. The retreat's purpose was to furnish writers with favorable working conditions, solitude, emotional support, artistic freedom, and egalitarianism. In 1949, an ugly skirmish erupted when a small number of Colony residents led by Robert Lowell denounced Ames because she had permitted an author with Communist sympathies to reside at the retreat. They contended that her actions were unacceptable and that she should be fired. In response, several writers came to her rescue, among them Glenway Wescott, who, although not a Yaddo artist-in-residence, nevertheless dispatched an indignant letter to the Colony's Board of Directors in which he advised, in the strongest of terms, that Ames be retained and her antagonists reprimanded.

"Lowell and the others are the troublemakers," he told the directors. "I wish they might be not only controverted and rebuffed but formally reproved by your meeting for repaying Mrs. Ames's kindness and toleration with their presumption and self-assurance and spite."[44]

In the end, Ames was allowed to remain in her post. In fact, she continued as the colony's executive director for the next twenty years, displaying exemplary leadership throughout her tenure. She was deeply grateful to Westcott for his intervention, appreciation she expressed in a heartfelt letter after the dispute was resolved.

Wescott's efforts to advance the ideals of freedom of thought and freedom of expression persisted after the Yaddo incident. In the 1950s, he became involved in an organization based in Paris and financed secretly by the Central Intelligence Agency. Known as the Congress for Cultural Freedom, it was a covert operation whose mission was to support non-Communist left-wing American writers, artists, and scholars in an effort to counter mounting Soviet cultural influence in the West. William Faulkner, Tennessee Williams, W. H. Auden, and a handful of other authors were also involved, with Wescott being a featured speaker at the Congress's 1952 symposium in Paris.

As to their knowledge of the CIA's role in the affair, while it was not exactly an open secret among American writers, it has been reported that "a large number suspected Agency involvement."[45] At least one participant, the poet Allen Tate, was clearly aware of its presence, which he disclosed in a letter to a friend.[46] It is uncertain if Wescott knew about the CIA connection, although he did refer to himself as a "propagandist" in a journal entry written in Paris during his 1952 visit.[47] It may have been the case, then, that his views were so firmly anti-Communist that he was not all that troubled by the Agency's sponsorship, assuming he was aware of it.

Wescott was elected President of the National Institute of Arts and Letters in 1959, and remained in the post until the mid-1960s. He took this role very seriously, using it to strengthen and promote the American arts community. Among other actions, he conveyed to President Kennedy the need for increased federal funding for writers and artists on the grounds that the nation had much to gain by supporting its existing pool of talent and fostering the development of those with potential. He also championed the rights of authors, and on several occasions mediated complicated literary disputes. Despite being perceived by the public as a prim, even a quaint, literary figure during this increasingly radical era, Wescott won the admiration of liberals and conservatives alike for his efforts.

During this same period, the late 1940s through the mid-1960s, Wescott also became acquainted with a large number of gay and lesbian authors who he met through his activities at the National Institute or through mutual friends. The latter occurred with increasing frequency after he and Wheeler leased a swank Park Avenue apartment. George Platt Lynes was still residing on the West Coast at this time and would never live with the couple again.

At their new address, Wescott and Wheeler entertained often, as well as being among the A-list guests of several important Manhattan socialites. Wescott's memoirs, as well as biographers' accounts of his life during this period, reveal that he rubbed shoulders with such notables as Cecil Beaton, Leonard Bernstein, Truman Capote, Aaron Copland, Isek Dinesen (Karen Blixen), Somerset Maugham, and Gore Vidal. He was also on cordial terms with Brooke Astor, Dorothy Parker, Diana Vreeland, and the Baroness Pauline de Rothschild, whom he had befriended several years before she married into profound wealth. In addition, he was a comrade-in-arms of Alfred Kinsey, the intrepid investigator of human sexual behavior.

The Institute for Sex Research

Kinsey, a distinguished fifty-five-year-old researcher when he made the acquaintance of the forty-eight-year-old Wescott, had obtained a doctorate in biology at Harvard in 1919, then accepted a teaching position in zoology at Indiana University. In 1938, the university asked that he add a class in marriage to his course load, and it was his preparation for this task that altered the direction of his career. Kinsey encountered a glaring lack of factual information about human sexuality as he gathered materials for the course and thus took it upon himself to begin interviewing an array of men and women to build a meaningful knowledge base. He succeeded and by 1947, his investigations had become so fruitful that the university established a nonprofit facility, the Institute for Sex Research, and appointed him director, with principal funding provided by the Rockefeller Foundation. During the next several years, Kinsey and his associates used this funding wisely, interviewing an estimated 18,000 people about their sex lives, producing films and publishing books on sexual topics, and in many other ways contributing to the public understanding of the varieties of human sexual experience.

The bond between Wescott and Kinsey was formed in the spring of 1949 when the researcher visited the Museum of Modern Art in Manhattan. There, Wheeler arranged for him to interview several renowned painters about their erotic histories in an effort to expand the Institute's range of participants. Naturally, Wheeler told Wescott about Kinsey and his groundbreaking studies at this time, and Wescott, intrigued, invited the researcher to a small dinner party. The other guests included Christopher Isherwood and E. M. Forster, Forster's policeman-boyfriend Bob Buckingham, and mythologist Joseph Campbell, a gathering that made quite an impression on the researcher. Following a spirited dinner conversation, Kinsey invited his host to visit the Institute in Bloomington, Indiana, and Wescott took him up on the offer a few months later. It would be the first of many such visits.

Wescott quickly became attached to Kinsey, who exuded a positive, liberated attitude toward sex that helped the writer better accept his own sexual nature. Kinsey also believed in the need for public awareness and frank discussion of homosexuality, a view shared by Wescott. Indeed, Wescott purportedly planned to write a book at this juncture in which he would reveal his own same-sex disposition, but unfortunately failed to see the project through to completion. Even so, his many other deeds for Kinsey and the Institute no doubt compensated for any books he did not finish, deeds that were sometimes rather audacious.

On one occasion, for instance, Wescott held a gay sex party at his Manhattan apartment so the researcher could observe firsthand an assortment of men having sex together. As the guests made love, Kinsey strolled through the rooms watching them studiously. The author also allowed himself to be questioned at length about his own sexual background and ensured that his friends and colleagues, male and female, likewise permitted themselves to be interviewed. According to biographer Jerry Rosco, Wescott even permitted the Institute's photographer to film him in a solitary sex act as part of an assemblage of explicit research films the center was creating. And these were not his only contributions. At Kinsey's request, Wescott read countless volumes of erotica, then helped select those to be included in the Institute's library. He further helped Kinsey prepare for publication the ground-breaking book, *Sexual Behavior in the Human Female,* a follow-up to the researcher's 1948 classic, *Sexual Behavior in the Male.* This latest text contained new information about homosexuality that Wescott was eager to see in print. After his 1952 appearance at the International Congress of Cultural Freedom in Paris, Wescott traveled to Rome, where he smuggled nearly a hundred erotic drawings back to the United States and donated to the Institute. He made certain that George Platt Lynes donated several nude photographs as well.

To be sure, Wescott contributed appreciably to Kinsey's pioneering efforts, particularly to his studies on gay sexuality. At least twice a year during the early 1950s, he visited the scientist at the Indiana facility, as well as conferring with him when Kinsey came to Manhattan, all the while offering staunch moral support. This was perhaps most evident when the researcher's work came under fire from conservative Republicans during the McCarthy era, politically motivated attacks that prompted the Rockefeller Foundation to withdraw its financial support. It was at this point that Kinsey, distraught over the loss of funding and weakened by the persecution he was enduring, began suffering heart attacks, one of which occurred at Wescott's apartment. Before long, the strain proved too much, and Kinsey died in 1955. Not surprisingly given their bond, Kinsey's demise wounded Wescott deeply, particularly since it occurred only a few months after the death of George Platt Lynes, who had returned to Manhattan in dire financial straits with a diagnosis of lung cancer. Wescott, always the loyal friend and lover, had been at Lynes's hospital bedside when the photographer passed away.

In the years following the loss of these two cherished comrades, Wescott continued working with the staff at the Institute for Sex Research on an intermittent basis, as well as remaining friends with Mrs. Kinsey. He also held firmly to his belief in the need for objective research into gay sexuality.

SUNSET AT HAYMEADOWS

In the 1960s, Wescott, now an elderly man, lived in New Jersey on his brother's new farm, Haymeadows, where he and Wheeler adopted the estate's rustic stone millhouse and made it their home. Wescott also sought to remain involved in the literary world, publishing a book of essays, *Images of Truth,* in which he described the personal qualities of six fellow writers, most of whom were also his friends, and critiqued their work. Among those he honored in this manner were Colette, Isak Dinesen, Thomas Mann, Somerset Maugham, Katherine Anne Porter, and Thornton Wilder.

In addition, he labored over his journals, published posthumously under the title, *Continual Lessons*. In them, Wescott recounted with striking candor some of his earlier sexual escapades, as well as using the opportunity to reiterate his long-standing opposition to the concept of gay male monogamy. "I have come to the conclusion that for most males the two-person pattern is just an ideal, an imposed discipline, a convention, a hypocrisy, a phase or episode . . . short-lived, one-sided, anguished, laborious, wearisome," he wrote.[48]

Wescott also wrote nonfiction pieces for newspapers and magazines, and, within certain limits, stayed active in major literary organizations, most notably PEN and the National Institute of Arts and Letters. When his stamina cooperated, he also gave interviews, such as the one he granted Frank Gado, an English professor at Union College, in which Wescott expressed his wish that his body of work prove beneficial to others. "I would hope that everything I wrote would be helpful, useful to somebody," he told Gado.

> Although I don't know that I always write with a view to making helpful suggestions, or to teaching a lesson, or anything of that sort, I'm a real believer in truth-telling and truth-hearing as an exercise for the mind. It's the most difficult thing in the world to tell the truth, and it's very difficult to recognize the truth—but very important that people do.[49]

The aging writer struggled to stay abreast of the social change that was occurring at breakneck speed during the latter half of the century. Monroe Wheeler, as always, remained Wescott's one abiding soul mate, but with John Stevenson, his new and considerably younger companion, he attended readings of avant-garde poetry, parties, and the occasional rock concert, while also visiting friends on Fire Island. As well, he kept an eye on the burgeoning gay liberation movement, although, like many older gay men, he was uncomfortable with its more provocative elements. Nevertheless, Wescott retained his belief in the need for the legal right to love those of the same gender.

In his lifetime Wheeler had succeeded in distinguishing himself as an important authority in the visual arts, having been awarded the Legion of Honor by the French government for his work on behalf of modern French painters. After retiring from the Museum of Modern

Art, he also continued to serve in an honorary capacity on the museum's Board of Directors. Even in his advanced years, Wheeler stayed remarkably active, with his art projects taking him to far-flung sites in Asia and Latin America. Toward the end, however, he seemed to derive the greatest satisfaction simply by staying at Haymeadows with his beloved Wescott and the affectionate cats that roamed the estate. It was here, in the New Jersey countryside, that the couple's time together inevitably came to a close.

In 1986, Wescott suffered a stroke that required him to be hospitalized for several weeks and left him impaired. Upon returning to Haymeadows, Wheeler created a ground-floor bedroom in their library for the infirm writer, where Wescott lived, for months on end, amid the books he loved. Then, on Valentine's Day the following year, he suffered another stroke which claimed his life. It was a peaceful conclusion to a vibrant existence.

In his will, Wescott left all of his possessions to Wheeler, who was himself in poor health. Indeed, he, too, passed away shortly afterward. In all, the couple had been together for nearly seven decades, during which time they had sometimes squabbled, more often loved, and always prevailed. And they had done far more: the pair had contributed immeasurably to the fields of art and literature, thereby enriching twentieth-century culture. As noted at the beginning of this account, Wescott's name has faded in the years since his demise, which is regrettable because he was such a gifted writer, as well as a gay man who made persistent efforts to enhance the public's awareness and acceptance of the homosexual citizenry. It is imperative that Glenway Wescott be remembered for the exceptional figure that he was: the author, the elder statesman, and the politically progressive member of a disfavored minority who used his life to enlighten the society of his day.

NOTES

1. Sontag, Susan, *Where the Stress Falls* (New York: Farrar, Straus and Giroux, 2001, p. 11).

2. Wescott, Glenway, Phelps, Robert, with Rosco, Jerry, eds., *Continual Lessons: The Journals of Glenway Wescott* (New York: Farrar, Straus and Giroux, 1990, p. ix).

3. Wescott in Rosco, Jerry, *Glenway Wescott, Personally: A Biography* (Madison, WI: University of Wisconsin Press, 2002, p. 6).

4. Millett, Fred, *Contemporary American Authors: A Critical Survey and 219 Bio-Bibliographies* (New York: Harcourt, Brace and Company, 1940, p. 631).

5. Wescott, Glenway, *Images of Truth* (New York: Harper & Row, 1962, pp. 15-16).

6. Wescott, in Rosco, *Glenway Wescott, Personally: A Biography,* p. 19.

7. Kolata, Gina, *Flu: The Story of the Great Influenza Pandemic of 1918 and the Search for the Virus That Caused It* (New York: Farrar, Straus and Giroux, 1999).

8. Wescott, in Rosco, *Glenway Wescott, Personally: A Biography,* p. 17.

9. Ibid., p. 16.

10. Rueckert, William, *Glenway Wescott (Twayne's United States Authors Series)* (New York: Twayne Publishers, Inc., 1965, p. 25).

11. Rood, Karen, ed., *Dictionary of Literary Biography,* Volume IV: *American Writers in Paris, 1920-1939* (Detroit: Gale Research Company, 1980, p. 403).

12. Fitch, Noel Riley, *Sylvia Beach and the Lost Generation: A History of Literary Paris in the Twenties and Thirties* (New York: W. W. Norton, 1985, p. 194).

13. Rood, *Dictionary of Literary Biography.*

14. Ernest Hemingway, in Wescott, Phelps, and Rosco, *Continual Lessons,* p. xiii.

15. Hemingway, Ernest, *The Sun Also Rises* (New York: Scribner, 1954, 1926, p. 29).

16. Carpenter, Humphrey, *Geniuses Together: American Writers in Paris in the 1920s* (Boston: Houghton Mifflin, 1988, p. 29).

17. Gertrude Stein, in Benfry, Christopher, Book Review of *Bright Young Things: The European Years of George Platt Lynes, Monroe Wheeler and Glenway Wescott, Documented in Photographs* by Anatole Pohorilenko and James Crump (March 21, 1999). *The New York Times* Web site <www.nytimes.com/books/99/03/21/reviews/99/03/21/reviews/990321.21benfyt.html>, p. 1.

18. Gertrude Stein, in Carpenter, *Geniuses Together,* p. 69.

19. Johnson, Ira, *Glenway Wescott: The Paradox of Voice* (Port Washington, NY: National University Publications, 1981, p. 41).

20. Wescott, Glenway, *The Grandmothers* (New York: Arbor House, 1986, 1927; p. 374).

21. Wescott, Glenway, *Good-Bye Wisconsin* (New York: Harper & Brothers, 1928, p. 95).

22. Ibid., p. 302.

23. Rueckert, *Glenway Wescott,* p. 46.

24. Millett, *Contemporary American Authors,* p. 631.

25. Wescott, in Rosco, *Glenway Wescott, Personally: A Biography,* p. 53.

26. Wescott, Glenway, Dedication in *Fear and Trembling* (New York: Harper & Brothers, 1933).

27. Bawer, Bruce, *Diminishing Fictions: Essays on the Modern American Novel and Its Critics* (St. Paul, MN: Graywolf Press, 1988, p. 150).

28. Hemingway, in Rosco, *Glenway Wescott, Personally: A Biography,* p. 57.

29. Bawer, *Diminishing Fictions,* p. 149.

30. Chauncey, George, *Gay New York: Gender, Urban Culture and the Making of the Gay World, 1890-1940* (New York: Basic Books, 1994, p. 351).

31. Bawer, *Diminishing Fictions,* p. 149.

32. Margot Livesey, "The hidden machinery," in Conroy, Frank, ed., *The Eleventh Draft: Craft and the Writing Life from the Iowa Writers' Workshop* (New York: HarperCollins, 1999, p. 99).

33. Wescott, in Rosco, *Glenway Wescott, Personally: A Biography,* p. 172.

34. Estate of Glenway Wescott, "A visit to Priapus," in *The James White Review* 19(2/3) (2002): 42.

35. Ibid., 43.

36. Wescott, Glenway, *The Pilgrim Hawk* (New York: New York Review Books, 2001, 1940, p. 11).

37. Ibid., p. 13.

38. Ibid., p. 102.

39. Ibid., p. 21.

40. Rueckert, *Glenway Wescott,* p. 114.

41. Johnson, *Glenway Wescott,* p. 110.

42. Wescott, Glenway, *Apartment in Athens* (New York: Harper & Brothers, 1945, p. 237).

43. Ibid., p. 239.

44. Wescott, Phelps, and Rosco, *Continual Lessons,* p. 234.

45. Troy, Thomas M., Jr., undated Book Review of *Cultural Cold War: The CIA and the World of Arts and Letters* by Frances Stonor Saunders. CIA Web site <www.cia.gov/csi/studies/vol46no1/article08.html>, p. 1.

46. Foley, Barbara, *Renarrating the Thirties in the Forties and Fifties.* Rutgers University Web site <newark.rutgers.edu/~bfoley/foleyfifties.html>.

47. Wescott, Phelps, and Rosco, *Continual Lessons,* p. 330.

48. Ibid., pp. 318-319.

49. Glenway Wescott, in Gado, Frank, *First Person: Conversations on Writers and Writing* (Schenectady, NY: Union College Press, 1973, p. 30).

REFERENCES

Bawer, Bruce (1988). *Diminishing Fictions: Essays on the Modern American Novel and Its Critics.* St. Paul, MN: Graywolf Press.

Benfry, Christopher (March 21, 1999). (Book Review) *Bright Young Things: The European Years of George Platt Lynes, Monroe Wheeler and Glenway Wescott, Documented in Photographs* by Anatole Pohorilenko and James Crump. *The New York Times* Web site: <www.nytimes.com/books/99/03/21/reviews/990321.21benfyt.html>.

Carpenter, Humphrey (1988). *Geniuses Together: American Writers in Paris in the 1920s.* Boston: Houghton Mifflin.

Chauncey, George (1994). *Gay New York: Gender, Urban Culture and the Making of the Gay World, 1890-1940.* New York: Basic Books.

Fitch, Noel Riley (1985). *Sylvia Beach and the Lost Generation: A History of Literary Paris in the Twenties and Thirties.* New York: W. W. Norton.

Foley, Barbara (undated). *Renarrating the Thirties in the Forties and Fifties.* Rutgers University Web site: <newark.rutgers.edu/~bfoley/foleyfifties.html>.

Gado, Frank (1973). *First Person: Conversations on Writers and Writing.* Schenectady, NY: Union College Press.

Hemingway, Ernest (1954/1926). *The Sun Also Rises.* New York: Scribner (Simon and Schuster).

Johnson, Ira (1971). *Glenway Wescott: The Paradox of Voice.* Port Washington, NY: National University Publications.

Kolata, Gina (1999). *Flu: The Story of the Great Influenza Pandemic of 1918 and the Search for the Virus That Caused It.* New York: Farrar, Straus and Giroux.

Livesey, Margot (1999). The hidden machinery. In Conroy, Frank (Ed.), *The Eleventh Draft: Craft and the Writing Life from the Iowa Writers' Workshop* (pp. 85-100). New York: HarperCollins.

Millett, Fred (1940). *Contemporary American Authors: A Critical Survey and 219 Bio-Bibliographies.* New York: Harcourt, Brace and Company.

Rood, Karen (Ed.) (1980). *Dictionary of Literary Biography,* Volume IV: *American Writers in Paris, 1920-1939.* Detroit: Gale Research Company.

Rosco, Jerry (2002). *Glenway Wescott, Personally: A Biography.* Madison, WI: University of Wisconsin Press.

Rueckert, William (1965). *Glenway Wescott (Twayne's United States Authors Series).* New York: Twayne Publishers, Inc.

Sontag, Susan (2001). *Where the Stress Falls.* New York: Farrar, Straus and Giroux.

Troy, Thomas M., Jr. (Undated). (Book Review) *Cultural Cold War: The CIA and the World of Arts and Letters* by Frances Stonor Saunders. Central Intelligence Agency Web site: <www.cia.gov/csi/studies/vol46no1/article08.html>.

Wescott, Glenway (1928). *Good-Bye Wisconsin.* New York: Harper & Brothers.

Wescott, Glenway (1933). *Fear and Trembling.* New York: Harper & Brothers.

Wescott, Glenway (1945). *Apartment in Athens.* New York: Harper & Brothers.

Wescott, Glenway (1962). *Images of Truth.* New York: Harper & Row.

Wescott, Glenway (1986, 1927). *The Grandmothers.* New York: Arbor House.

Wescott, Glenway (2001, 1940). *The Pilgrim Hawk.* New York: New York Review Books.

Wescott, Glenway, Estate of (1995). A visit to Priapus. In *The James White Review* (2/3): (Spring/Summer 2002): 39-43.

Wescott, Glenway, Phelps, Robert, with Rosco, Jerry (Eds.) (1990). *Continual Lessons: The Journals of Glenway Wescott.* New York: Farrar, Straus and Giroux.

AARON COPLAND

Aaron Copland, portrait (undated). (Photo by Don Perdue. Courtesy of Thirteen/ WNET New York.)

INTRODUCTION

Hailed by *The New York Times* as "the pioneer of American music,"[1] Aaron Copland, composer of the Pulitzer Prize–winning *Appalachian Spring,* was a man of principle and heart, a man whom a friend and former lover once described as among "the dearest, kindest, most thoughtful and fundamentally good human beings I've ever known."[2] Certainly it is true that the composer attracted a legion of admirers over the years for his integrity and generosity, as well as receiving an Academy Award, the Presidential Medal of Freedom, and the Congressional Gold Medal for his professional accomplishments. Yet Copland's life, despite its numerous high points, was not without its low ones, which is so often the case for those who find themselves visited by fame.

In the 1950s, the mild-mannered New Yorker was ordered to appear before Senator Joseph McCarthy to be interrogated about his political activities. McCarthy was convinced that Copland was a Communist sympathizer. Then there was the controversy surrounding his sexual orientation: Copland conducted himself as an openly gay man at a time when other homosexual celebrities struggled frantically to conceal their sexual dispositions. Because of his forthrightness in this regard, and especially because of his support of young gay musicians, he became the target of criticism by heterosexual musicians. The conductor was also maligned because of his Jewishness; specifically, he was accused of favoring Jewish colleagues in the profession. Such obstacles notwithstanding, Copland managed to scale great heights in the course of his lifetime, winning the public's admiration and affection through his warmheartedness and diplomacy, as well as establishing himself as the United States' best-known, and arguably its finest, composer of twentieth-century classical music.

This biography explores Copland's childhood in a large and loving family, his formative musical training in Paris, and his ensuing same-sex romances. His tenure as America's foremost composer is examined, with special attention to his sexual disposition and its impact on his career. The result should be a deeper understanding of this innovative artist whose work placed American orchestral compositions on a par with those of other nations and whose personal and professional integrity served as a model for generations of composers and musicians.

BROOKLYN DAYS

Born to Russian-Jewish immigrants on November 14, 1900, in Brooklyn, New York, Aaron was the fifth and final child in the Copland family. His parents, Harris and Sarah, owned and operated a successful department store in the heart of the borough, a business that, at its height, required a dozen employees. On the three floors above the store the family and its servants lived in comfort. The building was a mere ten-minute walk from the Brooklyn Museum of Art and the Brooklyn Academy of Music. Despite the Coplands' proximity to art and music, they did not steep themselves in culture as much as in commerce. The family business occupied the lion's share of their time and attention because Harris and Sarah, concerned about their relatives who had stayed behind in Russia, used its proceeds to bring them, one by one, to America.

Young Aaron enjoyed his early years in the Copland household, remembering them as a flurry of activity, affection, and, at times, religious celebration. Although the Orthodox family did not immerse itself in doctrine, the Coplands observed all of the major Jewish holidays, with Harris serving as president of the local synagogue for two years. It was because of Aaron's upbringing in such a milieu that he acquired a smattering of Hebrew and Yiddish along with a fondness for traditional Jewish music, which captivated him whenever he attended weddings or bar mitzvahs with his parents. This is not to say that all of the Coplands were drawn to music, however. Harris, for one, had little interest in it, tending instead to be "all business." Sarah and the children nicknamed him "The Boss" because of his no-nonsense demeanor.[3]

Harris was a serious, exacting man, but he was also a dedicated father who worked tirelessly to ensure that his children had every advantage. Concerned about their growth and maturation, he took it upon himself to arrange experiences for them that he believed would help bring about their proper development. He once took Aaron, as an adolescent, to Minsky's Burlesque and then to a bathhouse, a night on the town that electrified the youth and sparked in him the beginnings of a sexual awakening. Yet despite such indelible father-son moments,

Aaron was strongly attached to Sarah. "She was more sensitive than my father," he explained.[4] She was also more indulgent of Aaron's interest in music, as well as that of her other children.

Although the Copland household could not be described as overflowing with music, Aaron's older brother Ralph studied the violin with a renowned German virtuoso. His sister Laurine received vocal training at the Metropolitan Opera School and a private instructor also gave her piano lessons in the family's home. During these sessions eight-year-old Aaron would linger about the piano in an effort to snatch whatever information he could for himself, a cagey tactic that soon paid off. Within months, he had composed his first song, and before long had so impressed his sister with his talent that she offered to give him piano lessons so he could learn the instrument more efficiently. Finally, when it became evident that Aaron was displaying the attributes of a bona fide prodigy, Harris and Sarah arranged for him to study with a professional pianist. Through this course of events, the youngest Copland came to be an accomplished musician, debuting at the age of seventeen in a recital staged inelegantly at a Manhattan department store.

During his teenage years Copland began to recognize his attraction to other young men. Although he was unaware of his same-sex orientation prior to adolescence—typical of the era, his family never discussed the subject of homosexuality—Copland has said that he felt different from other boys, that he was "delicate by comparison."[5] By his own account, he became acutely aware of his lack of masculinity when he attended summer camp in upstate New York, where his shortcomings as a sportsman, in particular, were visible to everyone. Certainly no one mistook him for an athlete. Even so, the other youths admired his intelligence and judgment, and always sought his opinion on matters of importance. Furthermore, they genuinely liked him. Copland's easygoing nature won them over in the same way that it appealed to people throughout his lifetime. As to whether he experimented sexually with the other campers during these summer expeditions, or, for that matter, with other boys back in Brooklyn, he never mentioned it in interviews or in his memoirs.

His dedication to music solidified as he matured. At the age of seventeen, he began a three-year course of study in composition with Rubin Goldmark, nephew of Austro-Hungarian composer Karl Goldmark and former pupil of Anton Dvořák. Goldmark proved to be an inspiration and a guiding light, instructing Copland in the elements of harmony and counterpoint and helping him compose waltzes, scherzos, and sonatas. Goldmark would go on to head the Composition Department at The Juilliard School when the institution was founded a few years later, while Copland would seek out other notable teachers as he expanded and refined his skills.

After graduating in 1917 from Boys High School in Brooklyn, Copland decided to pursue private instruction rather than attend college. Accordingly, he continued his composition studies with Goldmark and added keyboard lessons from Clarence Adler, a renowned pianist whose other students included the promising young composer Richard Rodgers. To finance his studies, Copland played the piano in dance bands in the Catskill Mountains—the so-called Borscht Belt—and at various Brooklyn venues, performances that not only helped him earn money but also introduced him to intriguing musical styles, most notably jazz. They also brought him into contact with potential boyfriends.

While performing at the Finnish Socialist Hall in Brooklyn, he met a young Scandinavian cellist and fervent socialist, Arne Vainio. The two hit it off at once and before long were spending countless hours poring over copies of the *Call,* a leading socialist newspaper, and debating leftist politics and matters of musical interest. It is not known for certain whether they became lovers, although they were by all accounts very close. Howard Pollack, in his biography of the composer, notes that Copland wrote a lyrical piece for piano and cello at this time, *Poème,* and suggests that it may have been inspired by Copland's love for Vaino. Interestingly, the following year Copland created another piece for piano and cello, *Lament,* which incorporated a traditional Hebrew melody. From the timing and themes of these two works, it is possible that he was exploring elemental aspects of himself through music, namely, his attraction to other men and his Jewishness. One thing we do know is that the young composer had a pair of important experiences shortly thereafter that altered the course of his life, both personally and professionally.

In the first of these, Copland suffered a crisis in sexual identity at the age of twenty, an emotional storm brought on by the realization that he was irrevocably gay. The result: he decided that his sexual orientation was a natural manifestation of his genetic makeup and wholly accepted it.

In the second, he decided to leave his home in Brooklyn to pursue composition training in France, unabashedly telling his friends that he hoped to become a well-known figure in the music world. With this goal in mind, he applied to, and was accepted by, the newly established American Conservatory of Music in Fontainebleau situated forty miles south of Paris. He arranged to attend its inaugural session, which was to be held during the summer of 1921 at the Chateau de Fontainebleau, an imposing castle that had housed French royalty for four centuries. After completing the summer session, he planned to settle in Paris, where he would acquire further musical training. So it was that the fledgling composer boarded an ocean liner in New York Harbor with a steamer trunk and a tin of candy for the eight-day trip to Le Havre, France.

LIFE IN FRANCE

The voyage itself proved memorable, even a bit prophetic. Although Copland spent the first few days alone and seasick, by the end of the trip he had befriended several Frenchmen, among them an artist and a priest who taught him useful phrases in their language. He also struck up a friendship with a violinist with whom he practiced the piano in the ship's first class section each day. Copland's command of the piano was so impressive that he was invited to perform a solo on the last night of the voyage for a gathering of 400 passengers. During the performance he again became seasick. Copland was the only person in the opulent ballroom not dressed in formal attire. This was because he had none, but no one seemed to notice or care. His performance was all that anyone noticed, a presentation so stunning it made the pages of the *New York Herald*.

A few days later, ensconced in the Chateau de Fontainebleau, Copland set to work studying composition and conducting. At least once a week, he also wrote long letters to his parents brimming with warmth and good humor, and during his leisure moments bicycled with friends through the local forests. Most of all, though, he spent his hours at the Conservatory steeped in his studies. Although his three months at the school did not prove to be as valuable as he had anticipated—Copland discovered that he was more advanced than the other students—his stay was not without certain benefits. It was while he was at the Conservatory, for instance, that he met Nadia Boulanger, who later played a crucial role in his career. It was also at Fontainebleau that he heard his compositions performed before a general audience for the first time. The public response was so positive that he harbored doubts about the quality of his work. He feared its popularity might bespeak its inferiority, a concern that proved unfounded.

At the end of the summer session, closing concerts were staged at the Academy in Fontainebleau, as well as in the nation's capital at the imposing Paris Conservatoire, where the twenty-year-old's compositions topped the bill. Exhilarated, he wrote to his parents and furnished them with all of the details, including the fact that he would be performing five of his own piano pieces. "The last one is based on two jazz melodies, and ought to make the old professors sit up and take notice!" he joked.[6] In fact, French audiences did take notice, and not only because of his inspired attempts to fuse traditional methods and modern jazz. More generally, the public appreciated his bold efforts to inject life and energy into twentieth-century classical music.

During the autumn of 1921, concerts featuring Copland's avant-garde works continued to be staged in France, one of which boasted a performance by a celebrated American tenor. Adding to Copland's luster, M. Durand, the world's most prestigious music publisher, released one of the composer's piano pieces, *The Cat and the Mouse (Scherzo Humoristique)*. The influential publisher also invited him to his home for a visit. Copland, after only five months abroad, was on the rise.

During this same season he moved into a three-room apartment on the Left Bank with his cousin, fellow expatriate Harold Clurman. An aspiring dramatist, Clurman would eventually direct plays on Broadway, win acclaim as a drama critic, and with Lee Strasberg, form the renowned Group Theatre. At this early date, however, he was still an unknown artist who treasured his days with Copland and their third-floor walk-up. Clurman recalled that they lived a half-block from a sidewalk café where they rubbed shoulders with the bearded bohemians who sat at its tables absorbed in talk of poetry and socialism. The two men also explored Paris on foot. "We were very serious about the arts," Clurman says, "but we had a lot of fun too, going around to places like Sylvia Beach's bookstore and catching glimpses of famous writers like Hemingway, Joyce, and Pound."[7] In his later years,

Clurman would remember Copland as "careful, judicious, balanced," words that would be used to describe the composer throughout his lifetime.[8]

Clurman, although heterosexual, had an abiding affection for his cousin and accepted the composer's gayness without reservation. He was also comfortable with Copland's European lovers, men whose continental charm the composer found captivating. Music remained Copland's first love, and for this reason his expatriate years, because they centered almost entirely on music, proved to be among the most meaningful and gratifying of his life. Certainly, he was not alone in this respect.

During the 1920s, the "Jazz Age" in France, scores of composers from the United States traveled abroad to experiment with new forms of musical expression. In the same way that American writers flocked to France hoping to find inspiration on foreign soil, so young composers made the journey to study European musical traditions, then move beyond them. Copland was such an artist, remarkably open to new sounds and experiences. Whereas he had held the work of impressionist Claude Debussy close to his heart while living in the United States, after a few months in France he came to favor the modernists, such as neoclassicist Igor Stravinsky. He also gained exposure to, and an appreciation of, the anguished creations of Gustav Mahler and the elegant, haunting offerings of Gabriel Fauré. Copland was in an ideal position to familiarize himself with an array of composers and their works, and he did not squander the opportunity. Most nights of the week he attended concerts and whenever possible took in ballets, operas, plays, and films as well, often with Harold Clurman in tow. The principal force in Copland's musical education was Nadia Boulanger, who taught him harmony and composition.

As noted earlier, Boulanger was a faculty member of the American Conservatory of Music in Fontainebleau during the summer Copland was in residence and would go on to serve as its director. She would remain associated with the Conservatory in one capacity or another for the next fifty-eight years. In addition, she provided private instruction in her Paris studio, where she trained scores of American composers in the course of her long and distinguished career. Among her pupils were Leonard Bernstein, Marc Blitzstein, and Philip Glass. Quincy Jones was also a student, one whom Boulanger astutely steered away from conventional composition. "Go mine the ore you

already have," she told the gifted jazzman.[9] Boulanger regarded
Copland as a prized pupil and allowed him to study and practice at her
studio on a daily basis. She also invited him to dinner parties at her
apartment and to gatherings in her salon, where he met a host of contemporary artists. One such luminary was Igor Stravinsky, the "apos-
tle of modernism," in the words of music scholar Harold Schonberg.[10] "You cannot imagine the feelings of a young composer from
Brooklyn shaking hands with such a famous character," Copland said
after meeting Stravinsky.[11]

Boulanger was particularly intrigued by Copland's desire to create
music in a modern vein, and so she took it upon herself to enlighten
him on the manner in which traditional pieces, such as Bach's fugues
and preludes, were relevant to twentieth-century composition. She
believed it was important for Copland—indeed, for all budding composers who wished to pursue modern music—to study the past masters before setting off on their own. "Boulanger ranged brilliantly
over all of music literature," write Gail Levin and Judith Tick, "resur-
recting lost treasures of early music, like Monteverdi, reading through
a complex Mahler symphony score at the piano, and decoding the
prewar revolution wrought by Igor Stravinsky, whom she idolized."[12]
On numerous public occasions in subsequent years, Copland would
voice his gratitude to Boulanger for furnishing him with a rich musical background and for shedding light on the relationship between
traditional and nontraditional musical forms.

Besides schooling him in Western composition, Boulanger also
urged Copland to expand his abilities, at one point advising him to
compose a ballet score. Having little confidence in his skills in this
area, he initially scoffed at the idea, but with his mentor's continued
prodding decided to give it a try. He and Clurman traveled to Berlin
for inspiration, where they attended a showing of the film *Nosferatu.*
Afterward, Clurman penned a horror scenario based on the movie
while Copland composed the score. Although the outcome of their
collaboration, titled *Grohg,* would never be performed publicly, Boulanger regarded it highly nonetheless. A few years later, Copland returned to it himself, extracting elements of the score for use in his
Dance Symphony.

Although experiments such as *Grohg* proved beneficial to the
young composer, the most enduring effect of Copland's stay in Europe was the discovery of a desire within himself to create music with

a distinctly American flavor, an urge that grew out of his observation that the music of France was intimately tied to the French way of life. This realization came as somewhat of a surprise to Copland. As a boy growing up in a middle-class Brooklyn neighborhood, he had experienced classical music as detached from the hustle and bustle of daily life, not an organic part of it.

"Gradually, the idea that my personal expression in music ought somehow to be related to my own back-home environment took hold of me," he said.

> This desire to make the music I wanted to write come out of the life I had lived in America became a preoccupation of mine. . . . It was not so very different from the experience of other young American artists, in other fields, who had gone abroad to study in that period; in greater or lesser degree, all of us discovered America in Europe.[13]

Accordingly, Copland resolved to return to the United States and compose music drawn from the American experience.

THE MUSICALIZATION OF AMERICANA

In the autumn of 1924, the young composer sailed back to Manhattan where he leased a studio apartment on the Upper West Side amid such imposing institutions as Carnegie Hall and the Metropolitan Opera House. With the help of a Guggenheim fellowship—the first ever awarded in the field of music—he resumed composing, striving to make musical statements that were explicitly American. He was not alone in this endeavor despite being credited, even today, with touching off the trend toward the "musicalization of Americana" to use Quincy Jones' term.[14] Copland's forerunners included such figures as Virgil Thomson, a fellow expatriate and Boulanger protégé with whom he became acquainted while in Paris. Although the two men knew each other "they were never especially close, being very different in temperament and background," writes music critic Anthony Tommasini. Both were gay but "Copland had more inner peace, less shame about his sexuality," Tommasini adds.[15] In regard to music, Thomson was creating works reflecting the American experience years before Copland decided to do so, unique pieces that made use of religious hymns, ragtime melodies, and even domestic speech patterns. Furthermore, his work had a lasting impact on American composers. Decades later Leonard Bernstein praised Thomson for "the extraordinary influence his witty and simplistic music had on his colleagues, especially on Aaron Copland," and Copland himself publicly expressed his artistic debt to Thomson on several occasions.[16] This was significant, too, since Copland was not always so generous to other composers, at least not to those he felt lacked the proper credentials.

At the same time Thomson was composing works of Americana in France, on the other side of the Atlantic a talented young songwriter, George Gershwin, was likewise seasoning his works with American flourishes. Gershwin shared remarkable similarities with Copland: both men were in their mid-twenties, the sons of Jewish-Russian immigrants in Brooklyn, and former pupils of Rubin Goldmark. Both were also interested in incorporating domestic motifs into contemporary music. "But because of their similarities," writes Joan Peyser,

> Copland must have felt threatened by Gershwin's presence on the concert scene. To him this man was strictly Tin Pan Alley, a Broadway boor with a cigar, and he did not want to be tainted by that image because of his own commitment to the idea of European art.[17]

Accordingly, Copland decided to keep a distance from his Brooklyn colleague, a difficult act to pull off without appearing snobbish, as events in the music community would soon reveal.

The same year that Copland returned to Manhattan, Gershwin's *Rhapsody in Blue* premiered and took the world by storm. As a follow-up, Gershwin set to work on Concerto in F Major for Piano and Orchestra, a piece designed to capture the color and vibrance of the metropolis. It made use of blues melodies and jazz rhythms, and thus was considered innovative for its time. In 1925, the work premiered at Carnegie Hall and became the talk of the town.

Copland's *Symphony for Organ and Orchestra* debuted this same year, then in 1926 he premiered his own jazz-imbued creation, Concerto for Piano and Orchestra, performed by the Boston Symphony under the direction of Serge Koussevitzky, a friend from his Paris days. Many concertgoers appreciated the presentation, however some accused Koussevitzky of insulting them by conducting the piece, with one particularly acerbic critic describing Copland's use of jazz as "tantamount to barbarism."[18] Copland stoically endured his detractors' invective. Unfortunately, though, he did something else during this moment in the spotlight, something not nearly as commendable: he ignored the accomplishments of George Gershwin, conspicuously failing to acknowledge any inspiration he may have received from his rival's recent jazz-hued works. "Not a word about Gershwin," writes Rodney Greenberg.[19] This is not to say that Copland borrowed musical ideas from his fellow composer then refused to admit it. As noted, Copland had already infused jazz into the piano pieces he performed in Paris five years earlier. However, he apparently did not consider Gershwin a serious composer, serious enough to warrant mention, or perhaps he was simply trying to be polite by keeping his opinion to himself. Whatever the reason, he did not recognize Gershwin publicly at this time.

That said, in 1945 Copland did include the composer's name on a list of ten artists he considered "worthy to represent American culture to European nations."[20] He also conducted *Rhapsody in Blue* on several occasions, and in the 1970s referred to Gershwin as "a good Broadway composer" in response to a question from a Juilliard student.[21] Perhaps the most telling comment can be found in Copland's 1982 autobiography in which he writes, "In many ways Gershwin and I had much in common . . . (but) we moved in very different circles."[22] Ultimately, Copland's attitude toward Gershwin, which many continued to regard as elitist, "helped perpetuate the disappointment Gershwin bore all his life, in that his success . . . did not bring with it the recognition he craved from the American musical establishment," says Greenberg.[23]

George Gershwin died at the age of thirty-eight, the result of a brain tumor, whereas Copland's life and career proved much longer and more expansive. By the time he was in his early thirties, Copland had become a celebrity with distinction and it was now, secure in his professional standing, that he returned to making bold changes in his style. At this time he brought to an end the use of jazz in his compositions. "True, it was an easy way to be American in musical terms," he said, "but all American music could not possibly be confined to two dominant jazz models: the 'blues' and the snappy number."[24] He also began experimenting with abstractionism, an approach marked by the disharmonious and the austere, that led to such works as his *Piano Variations*. Because of such experimentation he attracted further at-

tention. Many young composers, referred to as Coplanites, adapted
his style for their own use and older composers christened him "Dean
of American Music."[25] Even in the face of such accolades, the de-
mure New Yorker retained his humility and continued being open and
accessible to others, particularly to other gay men, musicians or otherwise.

During this era, Copland began frequenting gay bars in Manhattan,
sometimes with Harold Clurman by his side. Although little is known
about the composer's activities in such locales, he did have liaisons
with other men, a few of whom were, or were to become, quite prominent. One such lover was musician and author Paul Bowles, who would
one day write the existential novel, *The Sheltering Sky.* Ten years
younger than Copland, Bowles studied composition under him and
evidently succumbed to his charm. It was to Bowles that Copland
stressed the value of self-discipline, on repeated occasions telling
him tongue-in-cheek, "If you don't work, by the time you're thirty no
one will love you."[26] Certainly this was a dilemma Copland would
never have to face. He always worked very hard, and at the age of
thirty-two embarked on the grandest romance of his life with a man
half his age.

Victor Kraft

The object of his affection was a violin prodigy named Victor Kraft
who had studied part-time at Juilliard while still in high school. Re-
cently graduated, the teenager was headed for a career as a musician
when he began instruction under Copland. By all accounts, the youth
was a stunner. Tall and stately, he had blue eyes, brown hair, and a
deep, resonant voice. His personality resembled Copland's in that he
was bright, good-humored, and kindly disposed toward others. Unlike the composer, however, Kraft was also moody, even tearful at
times, an instability that persisted throughout his lifetime. But when
Copland was first getting to know the youth, he was drawn to Kraft's
dynamic emotionalism and thus fell in love with him.

According to Howard Pollack, the composer and his protégé traveled to Mexico shortly after meeting, where Copland worked on a
new orchestral piece while acquiring a taste for Mexican folk music.
During their stay, the couple also enjoyed an intimate holiday in Aca-
pulco, during which a friend took photos of them on the beach em-

bracing playfully for the camera. Copland, a little out of character perhaps, took his turn with the camera as well, snapping nude shots of Kraft in suggestive poses. As such antics reveal, the pair was happy and carefree during their foreign sojourn, which lasted four months and made an indelible impression on both of them. Copland returned to Mexico on several occasions to explore in greater depth its indigenous music, with his visits culminating in such works as *El Salón México,* a masterful piece inspired by the country's boisterous music halls and dedicated to Kraft.

Upon returning to the United States, Kraft moved into Copland's New York apartment where the two lived together for the next decade. Given the era, their living arrangement was an audacious one; surely it was a rarity for an American composer of Copland's stature to share a home with a partner of the same gender, let alone such a young one. Copland and Kraft were in love, though, and thus were intent upon spending as much time together as possible.

The pair was well-known in Manhattan social circles, their age difference and homosexuality being largely accepted by those around them. Copland's friends, male and female, genuinely liked Kraft; all of them spoke highly of him and the youth admired these men and women in return. Kraft also found their professions intriguing, most of which centered on the arts and letters. It was through these friends that he acquired an interest in photography, one that led to a stint modeling for Cecil Beaton before getting behind the camera himself.

Kraft, with Copland's encouragement, decided to forgo a career as a violinist in favor of becoming a photographer, and within a few years was well on his way. Among other accomplishments, he worked as a photojournalist during the Spanish Civil War, and subsequently studied under Margaret Bourke-White. He also served as a photographer at *Harper's Bazaar,* although he eventually encountered problems with the magazine's management and left the job under bitter circumstances. Truth be told, Kraft was a good photographer but not a great one, and worse still, as he aged he became increasingly plagued with inner demons and impulsive behavior that made life difficult for himself and others.

One of those most affected was Copland, who, in the early 1940s, decided to dissolve his ten-year romance with the younger man. In part, this was because he discovered that Kraft had shared Leonard Bernstein's bed during a stay on the West Coast. As could be expected, Copland's trust diminished considerably, although he remained on more or less cordial terms with Kraft. "Even when Victor became difficult and demanding," writes biographer Vivian Perlis, "Copland would never abandon him."[27] Perlis's observation is supported by the fact that in the 1950s the composer agreed to serve as the godfather to a child Kraft sired, a boy named Jeremy Aaron, who was born with brain damage and had to be placed in a residential treatment center.

Kraft's own mental condition gradually deteriorated over the next three decades, and his behavior became increasingly erratic, impulsive, and flighty. He once abducted his son from the residential center, for instance, and traveled the globe with him. Kraft also lived in England for a time, where Copland visited him on occasion. In still another instance, Kraft showed up unbidden on the composer's doorstep and implored him to come away with him and live in a windmill. Finally, after wandering the world and dabbling in Communism, Catholicism, and the Quaker religion, Kraft settled into the counterculture lifestyle that was prevalent in the 1960s and early 1970s before dying unexpectedly of cardiac arrest. Of course, Copland was stunned by the death, but he is said to have coped well with it nonetheless. "Copland was sad, but he was never gloomy or brooding for long," writes Perlis.[28]

Still, there were those, Leonard Bernstein among them, who believed that Copland privately blamed himself for Kraft's tragic descent. Friends recalled that the composer felt that the younger man might have avoided mental problems had he pursued the violin, his first love, rather than photography as Copland had urged. Copland also worried that their prolonged affair may have led the impressionable Kraft away from heterosexuality, perhaps his true sexual orientation, thereby producing lifelong distress. Judging from Kraft's personality features as a young adult, however, it appears that the composer did nothing to hasten his deterioration. If anything, he had a stabilizing influence. Nevertheless, the sympathetic, conscientious Copland appears to have been unduly critical of himself when it came to his former lover's emotional and spiritual decline.

Fortunately for Copland, he never suffered such a precipitous descent himself, but instead retained his sanity, as well as his talent, into old age. His life was not always comfortable, though. From the late 1920s into the mid-1930s, a period that encompassed his early years with Kraft, he was financially strapped much of the time. To pay the bills, he wrote articles and performed concerts subsidized by wealthy patrons of the arts, as well as lectured. He also obtained a grant from RCA, accepted money from relatives, and taught part-time at Harvard and the New School for Social Research. In short, he did just about anything to earn a living, while working determinedly on several new pieces that tended toward the abstract. Among these works were the *Short Symphony* and the intriguing *Statement for Orchestra,* compositions constructed on absolute logic. "These were stripped-down scores, dissonant, percussive, powerful, abstract," writes Harold Schonberg. "Pattern and rhythm were the main preoccupation, much more than melody."[29]

Not surprisingly perhaps, such unusual creations failed to strike a chord with audiences in the United States, who were in the grip of the Great Depression. Instead, during this period of national demoralization, a widespread preference existed for more prosaic renderings, such as domestic folk music, along with folk art, from quilts to paintings to furniture. Clearly, the American people longed for a return to a simpler, more comforting era. They also preferred that their music offer hope or at least a respite from the emotional devastation brought on by the economic crisis; abstract compositions, with their intrinsic intellectuality, ignored this need. So it was that Copland, worried that he and other modern composers would soon be "working in a vacuum," decided to modify his style once more in an effort to make a deeper, more enduring connection with the populace.[30] "I felt that it was worth the effort to see if I couldn't say what I had to say in the simplest possible terms," he explained.[31] To this end, he set to work searching for meaningful material, which he eventually found in home-grown legends and time-honored statesmen, among other sources.

POPULIST

From the mid-1930s through the 1940s, Copland experienced an especially fertile period during which he created memorable works that reflected past and present life in the United States. Aaron's desire to be "American," write Levin and Tick, "was symptomatic of the period."[32] The composer was successful in his aim; his music, even today, stirs audiences with its echoes of the heartland. "When I listen to

(Copland's) music, I hear America," filmmaker Spike Lee has said in recent times.[33]

Copland's compositions during this period included a minor piano piece, *The Young Pioneers,* as well as the *Ballade of Ozzie Powell,* a work for chorus and piano based on a text by Langston Hughes. The *Ballade* centers on one of the Scottsboro Boys, Ozie Powell, a four-teen-year-old African-American youth and political victim of an incident that was still unfolding in the courts of Alabama at the time. In this disturbing episode, nine black youths were wrongly accused of raping two Caucasian girls on a Southern Railroad freight train. Because the defendants were African American, they were presumed guilty by the legal establishment, denied counsel, and subjected to bodily attack by angry citizens. Yearning for their deaths, a mob even tried to lynch them at one point, a nasty affair that required 100 National Guardsmen to restrain the throng. Understandably, such a dangerous cocktail of fury and injustice prompted demonstrations across the United States and in twenty-five other nations, until the State of Alabama at last agreed that the Scottsboro Boys could have legal representation. Unfortunately, such belated counsel was of little value to young Powell, who was shot in the head by a policeman while in custody. Copland, being a minority member himself—that is, gay and Jewish—grasped all too well the arrant bigotry of the whole affair. For this reason, he generously agreed to score Hughes' stirring one-act play, *Scottsboro Limited.*

Copland also composed *Billy the Kid* around this time, a ballet based on the infamous outlaw who was gunned down in the 1880s near the Pecos River in New Mexico. The project appealed to Copland because it was consistent with his desire to draw upon American legendry in his work. The scenario was written by Lincoln Kirstein and choreographed by Eugene Loring, with the final product fast becoming one of the most renowned ballets of the era. After completing the work, Copland extracted elements of it for use in the *Billy the Kid Suite,* a piece for orchestra and two pianos that contained such folksy segments as "The Open Prairie," "In a Frontier Town," and "Cowboys with Lassos." For a nation struggling to emerge from the drab destitution of the Great Depression, such homespun renderings were a welcome reprieve.

Additional Copland works from this era include the patriotic *Lincoln Portrait,* designed for narrator and orchestra, and *Fanfare for the*

Common Man, a two-minute display for percussion and brass that has come to be associated with the ideals of democracy. Still heard at public ceremonies today, the *Fanfare* has been performed at the International Olympic Games.

By all accounts, Copland's melodic modernism touched the publicly deeply, as well as impressing his fellow artists. One such admirer was choreographer Agnes DeMille, who invited him to write the score for her forthcoming ballet, *Rodeo.* A unique work, the scenario centered on a young woman—a cowpoke—who had always dressed in men's clothing until one day she met a handsome male wrangler who sparked her interest. To snag him, she suddenly began wearing dresses and bows. Copland told friends in jest that he latched onto the assignment because he was drawn to the prospect of good-looking men dancing in tight blue jeans. Copland's excitement about the ballet, moreover, was matched by that of the public. Premiering in 1942 in New York City and danced by the Ballet Russe of Monte Carlo, the ballet was a huge hit. From it, the resourceful composer fashioned *Four Dance Episodes from Rodeo* that featured such segments as "Hoe-Down," "Buckaroo Holiday," "Corral Nocturne," and "Saturday Night Waltz." Many contemporary critics consider *Rodeo* and its variants to be among his most American creations.

Appalachian Spring

As it stands, a ballet Copland composed two years later, *Appalachian Spring,* ultimately became his most popular accomplishment, as well as his most enduring gift to American society. Commissioned by choreographer Martha Graham, Copland initially had no idea the music he was creating would become associated with the Appalachian Mountains. As a working title, he called the piece simply *Ballet for Martha,* while Graham referred to it as *House of Victory.* It was a couple of years before she selected the title *Appalachian Spring,* a phrase she borrowed from a Hart Crane poem. In reality, the ballet had no relation to springtime in the mountains; Graham just liked the phrase, so she used it. For the remainder of his life, Copland would become amused whenever concertgoers would commend him for capturing the sense of fresh mountain air in his music, since this was wholly unintentional.

The story is situated in rural Pennsylvania during the Civil War era, with the principal characters consisting of an idealistic young farmer and his bride. Because the couple is on the threshold of a new life together, hope reigns supreme. Graham stipulated that the stage set be stark and symbolic, specifically "the framework of a doorway . . . a Shaker rocking chair with its exquisite bonelike simplicity, and a small fence that should signify what a fence means in a new country."[34] As she further developed the ballet, Graham increasingly emphasized the Shaker element because of its association with simplicity.

In perhaps his best-known act as a composer, Copland incorporated into the score an obscure Shaker hymn, *Simple Gifts,* thereby lending the ballet an air of bygone innocence. The hymn "expressed the unity of the Shaker spirit, was ideal for Martha's scenario and for the kind of austere movements associated with her choreography," Copland said. "I did not realize that there never have been Shaker settlements in rural Pennsylvania!"[35]

Interestingly, the composer had toyed with the idea of writing an opera about the Shakers only a few years before. It seems he had long been fascinated with the fading religious sect, one that believed in total dedication to God, asceticism, perfection in work, pacifism, community property, and equal rights for both genders and all races. Although Copland never wrote the opera, his decision to embed *Simple Gifts* into Graham's ballet served as his own personal tribute to the languishing religious order. Graham, by comparison, was far less impressed with the Shakers' tenets and lifestyle. Although she admired their self-discipline, she viewed the sect, first and foremost, as a cult.

Appalachian Spring opened in October 1944, at the Library of Congress in Washington, DC, and this time the critics did not dismiss the new Copland composition as "barbarism." Indeed, the following year it brought him the Pulitzer Prize in music. From the original ballet he subsequently fashioned *Appalachian Spring Suite,* a work that came to be conducted by numerous luminaries, among them his friends Serge Koussevitzky and Leonard Bernstein. A few years later, Copland again reworked the ballet into a piece called *Shaker Variations,* as well as four alternative versions, including those for small orchestra, full orchestra, and concert band. Today, *Appalachian Spring* remains the one work of American classical music most recognized by domestic audiences.

Besides composing ballets, Copland also experimented with new and different media during his populist period. He created pieces for broadcast radio such as *John Henry* and *Music for Radio,* more commonly known as *Saga of the Prairie.* He also wrote music for plays, including a composition for string orchestra for use in Irwin Shaw's *Quiet City,* along with incidental music for *Five Kings,* Orson Welles's adaptation of Shakespeare's chronicle plays.

The composer also wrote the music for several movies, most of which centered on life in the United States. Such scores, in his view, humanized the action on the screen. "Film music is like a small lamp that you place below the screen to warm it," he said.[36]

Copland's first endeavor of this type was the score for the film *Of Mice and Men,* based on John Steinbeck's novel about the plight of migrant workers in California's Salinas Valley. He next composed the music for *The City,* followed by *Our Town,* the Hollywood version of Thornton Wilder's play about the ordinary, yet extraordinary, events of everyday life in a small New Hampshire town. From the latter, the composer extracted *Our Town Suite* and *Our Town: Three Piano Excerpts.*

Two years later, Copland, still enamored with the film industry, released *Music for the Movies,* which consisted of elements drawn from his three previous scores and included such wholesome segments as "New England Countryside," "Barley Wagons," "Threshing Machines," and "Grovers Corners." He also scored *The Cummington Story,* a documentary depicting the resettlement of refugees, *The Red Pony,* an adaptation of Steinbeck's masterful story about the human spirit, and *The North Star,* a film about Nazi brutalities in Russia for which he was nominated for an Academy Award. Then, in 1949, the composer wrote the music for William Wyler's *The Heiress,* and this score did bring him the Oscar for Best Original Musical Score. The prestigious award also brought Copland worldwide attention, which delighted him since he was interested in other nations' music and wished to involve himself artistically at the international level.

Besides being heavily invested in creating music emblematic of the United States, the composer spent substantial time exploring the music of other countries, particularly that of Latin America, which had enchanted him since his first visit to Mexico with Victor Kraft. Accordingly, he wrote several foreign-flavored works at this juncture, among them *Danzón Cubano,* a Latin American sketch designed for twin pianos and premiered on the concert stage by Copland and Bernstein, and *Las Agachadas,* a choral work more commonly known as the "Shake-Down Song." He also represented the United States on extended educational and public relations tours to Latin America, as well as Italy, sponsored by the State Department.

Affairs of the Heart

From the foregoing, it is evident that the composer spent considerable time writing memorable music for concert stage, radio, and screen. Although he had a busy professional life, he still made room for an active love life. After breaking off his romance with Victor Kraft in the early 1940s, Copland began dating young men once again, virtually all of whom were intelligent, gifted musicians in their late teens or early twenties. They were often emotionally troubled as well, the predominant problem centering on sexual confusion, a condition that sometimes led to additional difficulties with drink and depression. Copland served as a source of support for these distraught souls, a nurturing, mentoring function well-suited to his personality. Erik Johns, a painter and modern dancer who was himself a live-in lover of the composer for a time, likened Copland's role to that of the classical Greek practice in which an older man guides a younger one in the ways of the world.

Copland's romances usually lasted a few months, although some endured for years. Among the more protracted were those he formed with Alvin Ross, a painter to whom he was introduced by Leonard Bernstein, and Paul Moor, an up-and-coming pianist.

Copland's affairs were also marked by the sexual latitude he now afforded his partners. Astutely, by the time he reached his middle years, Copland no longer counted on his lovers to be entirely faithful to him. He was well aware that robust young men might not possess the self-restraint necessary to limit themselves to one person. Copland was aware, too, that he was not as physically attractive as his partners. Indeed, he often compared his face to that of a giraffe. As well, he knew from experience that a certain type of ambitious musician might agree to an amorous relationship with him for the sake of professional advancement. Undeterred, Copland opened his heart to several young men with whom he nearly always remained on amiable terms long after their romances had come to an end. The truth is, he loved being in love and thus did not hesitate to immerse himself fully in his affairs. It should also come as no surprise, then, that he eschewed casual sex. Such encounters held little interest for him.

As for the relationship between his sexual orientation and his music, Copland once explained that he believed a connection existed between the two but said that it was hard to pin down. "Aaron felt that his sexuality was there in the music," says Erik Johns, but he believed it was "incidental to his major theme."[37] It would appear to be the case that whatever else may have emerged from the nexus of his sexuality and his art, Copland's love for men provided him with inspiration for his work. In one revealing anecdote, a friend recalled how the composer, who had written three symphonies, once watched as a handsome music student strolled past him at a conservatory. Appraising the young man's beauty, Copland said to his friend, "There goes my Fourth Symphony."[38] To be sure, the composer was stimulated on several levels by other men, much to the benefit of American music.

ORGANIZER

American music also benefitted from Copland's efforts to mobilize those in the profession, particularly struggling composers, in the 1930s and 1940s. Sensitive to the post-Depression focus on the worth and the needs of the populace, Copland, although neither a socialist nor a communist, worked diligently to bring together elements of the music world for artistic and economic purposes.

After visiting the Yaddo Artists Colony in Saratoga Springs, New York, for instance, he organized the retreat's first concert series featuring notable American composers. His intention was to assemble gifted figures in classical music as a means of nurturing their creativity and publicizing their achievements. He subsequently established the Young Composers Group, a coterie designed to advance the state of American composition and one that contained within its ranks a rarity for the era, a female composer named Vivian Fine. He next assumed a seat on the board of directors of the League of Composers, following which he formed the Young Composers Alliance. Having endured a long and painful financial struggle several years previously while attempting to write music, Copland believed that fledgling composers deserved a stronger voice in the operation of the music business. More to the point, he argued that composers, rather than executives, should be in charge of the industry, from publishing music to arranging concerts, and should profit accordingly. Thus, by establishing the Alliance he was taking an important first step in handing his colleagues greater control over their careers, as well as the prospect of enhanced financial security. Unfortunately, his well-intentioned efforts to organize the music community were not always welcomed by those in the profession itself.

After he joined the League of Composers, Copland was assailed in print by Virgil Thomson in an alarming display of anti-Semitism. Declaring that the organization was "from top to bottom Aaron's baby," Thomson denounced it as "the League of Jewish Composers."[39] Thomson further planned to write an article for *Modern Music* criticizing Manhattan's music community and naming thirteen Jews who controlled it—Copland, of course, was among those to be "exposed"— but the journal refused to print it. Undaunted, Thomson continued hurling accusations at the composer, and he was not alone in doing so. Gay composer John Cage joined him in raising the "Jewish question" in regard to "the Copland organization," and insinuated that the mild-mannered Copland had hijacked the League of Composers in order to control the city's music scene and thereby advance himself and his fellow Jews in the profession.[40] As a man wielding considerable influence, Copland now attracted the envy and wrath of less prominent composers, and their ill will was not always aimed at his religious background.

A small group of disgruntled composers in other parts of the country accused him of favoring New Yorkers, while heterosexual musicians charged him with preferential treatment of young gay men in the profession. These individuals failed to grasp that Copland was surrounded by New Yorkers, that they comprised his milieu, so it was only natural that he would select colleagues from this group with whom he most familiar. As for the complaint that he was partial to youthful gay musicians, Copland did prefer such men as lovers but did not restrict himself to helping them professionally while ignoring all others. He assisted a substantial number of men and women over the years, gay and straight alike. Nevertheless, he faced the recurrent and annoying allegation that he unduly supported those who were homosexual, which may have been due in part to the times themselves.

In New York City during this period, the late 1940s through the 1950s, rumors abounded about a "Homintern" in the arts, this being a cynical play on the term "Comintern," the name of an international communist organization of the day. Among the gay composers said to belong to this mythical clique were Marc Blitzstein, John Cage, Samuel Barber, and Leonard Bernstein. As could be expected, Copland's name was high on the list of suspects, which may have been because he was the city's preeminent composer and had lived openly with Victor Kraft for a decade, as well as dating a string of male musicians afterward. Certainly it would be difficult to imagine a gay cabal without Copland in the thick of it.

The innuendo pertaining to the composer's Judaism and homosexuality, however, was nothing compared to a damning rumor that surfaced at this juncture and had to do with his supposed Communist ties. In this latest gossip, Copland's detractors implied that he was disloyal to the cause of democracy, ugly hearsay that found a small but gullible audience during the Red Scare. Despite his history of creating patriotic works and representing the nation on government-sponsored tours abroad, Copland was officially maligned in 1953 when Joseph McCarthy ordered him to appear in Washington, DC, to face questions about his political activities.

The McCarthy Ordeal

A Republican senator from Wisconsin, McCarthy sought to make a name for himself by weeding out alleged Communist infiltrators in the federal government, as well as in the citizenry itself. During an infamous public appearance in West Virginia in 1950, the ambitious politico waved a piece of paper at the crowd, a document that has since been discredited by several knowledgeable sources, and claimed it was a roster of Communist subversives employed in sensitive positions in the United States government.

McCarthy subsequently maneuvered himself into the influential position of Chairman of the Senate's Permanent Subcommittee on Investigations, a cousin to the House Committee on Un-American Activities with which he was also involved. Routinely, he would drag before the Subcommittee a man or woman to interrogate, typically a high-profile public figure whose presence guaranteed abundant press coverage. In Gestapo fashion, he would drill the individual mercilessly with inappropriate and intrusive questions. If the person did not answer as the senator wished, or, worse still, flatly refused to cooperate, McCarthy would publicly brand the individual a Communist sympathizer or destroy in other ways the person's credibility and livelihood. In this fashion, entirely blameless citizens were bullied into complying with the council. It is easy to understand why the senator's opponents, which came to include *The New York Times* and President Eisenhower, accused him of assaulting character, creativity, and free thought. They were right.

Copland came to the attention of opportunistic "Red baiters" in the Republican Party because of a conference he had attended a few years earlier at the Waldorf-Astoria in Manhattan during which the actions of the federal government were discussed in less than glowing terms. In the course of this meeting, termed the *Cultural and Scientific Conference for World Peace,* numerous speakers defended the Soviet Union against the Cold War policies of the United States. Although Copland attended the conference merely to hear its discussions—he was not a Soviet supporter—his presence alone was sufficient to cause him to be labeled a Communist sympathizer. A similar fate awaited some of his fellow attendees, whose ranks included such personages as Albert Einstein, Dmitry Shostakovich, Arthur Miller, Lillian Hellman, and Thomas Mann.

Copland's background as an organizer in the music community further complicated matters. Not only had he formed several groups in the 1930s designed to protect composers' rights and financial interests, but he had also taken part in the Composers Collective, an organization said to have Marxist underpinnings. Of course, he had a great deal of company in this regard; a sizable swath of the American citizenry was drawn to leftist politics in the years subsequent to the Great Depression, especially men and women in the arts. McCarthy and his associates, however, ignored this fact. During their term in power, they viewed with suspicion any person who had ever contemplated an alternative political ideology, be it socialism and communism, not that the McCarthyites were entirely capable of distinguishing between the two systems.

In Copland's case, he had not formally adopted either ideology, although he was acquainted with many who had done so. He had also formed professional relationships with prominent Soviets, among them conductor Serge Koussevitzky who had been a citizen of Russia before the Revolution of 1917. As well, Copland had helped establish the American-Soviet Music Society, a guild designed to foster the sharing of musical knowledge between the United States and the Soviet Union at a time when the two nations were still on amicable terms. Now, these salutary acts came back to haunt him.

Also haunting the composer was a series of music lectures he had delivered at Harvard University in the early 1950s. McCarthy, it seems, viewed the time-honored institution with contempt because of its large number of intellectuals. He was threatened by well-informed, independent-minded people—"free thinkers"—who were unafraid to examine and challenge the status quo.

Then there was the fact that Copland was homosexual—gay citizens were considered dubious in those days—and Jewish, neither of which did anything to assuage McCarthy's doubts about the composer's integrity. In regard to the latter, "there was an evident quotient of anti-Semitism in the McCarthy wave of hysteria," says Arnold Forster, former general counsel of the Anti-Defamation League. "Jews in that period were automatically suspect. Our evaluation of the general mood was that the people felt that if you scratch a Jew, you can find a Communist."[41]

An excitable Republican representative from Illinois, Fred E. Busbey, accused Copland in January 1953 of endorsing a nondemocratic political ideology and consorting with Communists. Not only did Busbey voice his spurious charge, he also made sure it was entered into the *Congressional Record.* Shortly thereafter, it was reiterated and debated in the pages of *The New York Times,* much to the composer's dismay.

Predictably, the fallout was instant. Within days, a presentation of Copland's *Lincoln Portrait,* which was to have been performed at the inauguration of President Dwight Eisenhower, was canceled. Its abrupt removal from the program left the ceremony with no American music, an awkward state of affairs.

Next, Joseph McCarthy strong-armed the State Department into banning the exportation of all music composed by any American citizen suspected of having Communist ties. Unfortunately, this now applied to Copland, thanks to Busbey's accusation, meaning that the composer's entire canon of works was withdrawn from nearly 200 music libraries situated around the world. And he was not alone; the compositions of George Gershwin, Leonard Bernstein, Virgil Thomson, and other American composers were likewise banned.

For Copland, such despotic actions reached a peak in May 1953, when McCarthy, as mentioned earlier, sent him a telegram ordering him to appear before the Permanent Subcommittee of Investigations in Washington, DC. The composer was to be interrogated about his purported Communist links.

Copland responded by dispatching two impassioned letters declaring his innocence, one to President Eisenhower and the other to Senator McCarthy himself. In them, he explained that while he had, over the years, signed petitions and other documents supporting the protection of civil liberties, beyond this he had no significant political experience. Although his statement was basically true, Copland in fact held strong political convictions that were becoming stronger by the day. He simply did not express them in a proactive, assertive manner. The normally unflappable composer was infuriated that he was forced to travel to the nation's capital, along with his high-priced attorney, to account for his beliefs and actions.

The interrogation was conducted behind closed doors by McCarthy and his closeted gay subordinate, attorney Roy Cohn. Present, too, were several government lawyers and representatives of the State Department. The nerve-wracking session lasted two hours, during which McCarthy, seemingly oblivious to the composer's extraordinary body of work, affronted him repeatedly. Among other aims, the senator was determined to extract from Copland the names of State Department officials who had asked him to represent the United States on educational tours abroad. McCarthy simply could not believe that the agency would select someone like Copland, whom he recklessly described as a man with a history of "tremendous activity in Communist fronts," unless Communist operatives had infiltrated the Department and were running the show.[42]

Copland, in response, tried to set the record straight, explaining that the agency had been interested solely in his music, not in his politics, that he had been chosen because of his stature in the music profession. His answers, however, only triggered more questions from McCarthy and his underlings. So the tussle went, with the composer providing forthright replies in most instances, but at times declining to name names, answering questions with questions, and dancing deftly around precarious subjects. When asked point-blank if he was a communist sympathizer, for instance, Copland responded by saying, "I am not sure I would be able to say what you mean by the word 'sympathizer.'"[43] Roy Cohn repeatedly injected himself into the proceedings in a heavy-handed, unruly manner, and his intrusiveness prompted McCarthy to rein him in on several occasions.

When the proceedings at last drew to a close, Cohn announced that within a week Copland would be brought before the Subcommittee again to answer more questions, but this time it would be a public hearing. Naturally, the composer was shaken by this prospect, but he was also resolute in his opinion that the Subcommittee was abusing its power. "My conscience was clear," he wrote in his diary. "In a free America I had a right to affiliate openly with whom I please . . . and no one had the right to question those affiliations."[44]

In the succeeding days, Copland, his lawyer, and former lover Victor Kraft, scrutinized the initial hearing's transcripts so the composer would be in a stronger position to refute the Subcommittee's allegations when he returned for the next session. In all, they identified nearly a hundred factual errors, not to mention several deletions of material that, if left intact, would have presented McCarthy in an unflattering light.

The impending public hearing never took place, much to the relief of Copland and his supporters. Although he remained under subpoena for an extended period, he was never summoned to testify again, presumably because he was such an honorable and revered public figure. Indeed, the initial proceedings drew outcries from Copland supporters because he was a national icon. In some circles, he was even regarded as a symbol of the republic itself. Although he was not compelled to undergo further interrogation, he still suffered the unpleasant consequences of the original allegations for many years.

In 1955, for instance, the FBI launched an investigation of the composer in anticipation of filing fraud and perjury charges against him. The aim was to prove that he had lied to the Subcommittee. When the probe failed to turn up any evidence, the FBI quietly dropped it.

Adding insult to injury, Copland could not travel abroad without official permission. Because he remained under subpoena, his passport was essentially invalid. After prolonged negotiations, however, the government granted him a six-month travel permit, then, after still more months of talks, accorded him a one-year authorization. Ironically, such harassment impeded his ability to represent the United States, ostensibly the world's greatest democracy, in international events.

Furthermore, although Copland was fortunate not to hold a government position or a full-time academic appointment—he would have been jobless by this point—he nevertheless suffered professionally. Although it will never be known the number of concerts he was not invited to conduct or the lectures he was not asked to deliver, it is known that certain institutions no longer associated with him for fear of inviting the McCarthyites into their own backyards.

In 1953, the University of Alabama canceled an invitation for Copland to appear at a three-day composers' forum and the Hollywood Bowl rescinded an invitation for him to conduct the Los Angeles Chamber Orchestra. One year later, the University of Colorado canceled an invitation for him to lecture in its music department, sparking protests among faculty and students. Regardless, university officials held fast to their decision, no doubt fearing a retaliation from McCarthy's forces if they reversed it.

The rebuffs continued. Two years later, the Borough of Brooklyn decided not to award a citation to the composer despite the fact that its membership had voted to do so. A similar situation arose when the American Society of Composers, Authors, and Publishers (ASCAP) refused to confer upon him an award for excellence. Even Ed Sullivan, the wooden emcee, snubbed him, refusing to say that Copland had composed *Lincoln Portrait* when the piece was broadcast on national television.

Sadly, such difficulties persisted well into the 1960s. Anonymous letters protesting an upcoming Copland concert arrived at the offices of the Dallas Symphony Orchestra and affected plans for the event, while the American Legion of San Antonio formally opposed his appointment to a lectureship at the University of Texas. It would seem, then, that Senator McCarthy, despite the eventual collapse of his Subcommittee, his censure by Congress, and his death from cirrhosis of the liver a few years later, succeeded in marring Copland's reputation and sapping his spirits. Among other difficulties, the abusive senator caused him profound stress, obstructed his professional activities, and cost him exorbitant legal fees. It must be said, though, that the federal government, to its credit, strove in consecutive decades to undo the harm the autocratic politician had inflicted upon the composer, although not all of the damage could be repaired.

Copland returned to work shortly after the 1953 hearing, but the ordeal left him battered, embittered, and demoralized. Of the artist caught in such a menacing context, Copland has said, "throw him into a mood of suspicion, ill will, and dread that typifies the Cold War attitude and he'll create nothing."[45] Although the composer did continue to create, many music scholars today maintain that his finest works were composed before McCarthy's assault on his civil liberties. Although that may be true, in all likelihood another factor was primarily responsible for this state of affairs, which had nothing to do with the McCarthy inquisition itself.

INNOVATOR

A few years before his confrontation with the notorious senator, Copland began to modify his musical style once again. He moved away from the warm, melodious works of Americana that had made him famous in order to write leaner, more complex compositions not unlike some of his creations from the late 1920s and early 1930s. Several of these new works were based on the principles of serialism, a method that was popular in elite circles of the day. Serial music was not embraced by the general public, however, and Copland was well aware of this fact. He knew that such compositions would prove less accessible, and thus less palatable, to mainstream audiences, but he wrote them anyway. It was mainly for this reason that the concert-going public lost interest in many of his post-McCarthy compositions. Audiences simply did not understand, or appreciate, serialism.

During this period, the 1950s through the 1960s, Copland's compositions included the *Canticle of Freedom, Inscape,* and *Connotations,* the latter commissioned by the New York Philharmonic for the opening of what is today Avery Fisher Hall at Lincoln Center. Other compositions included the *Piano Fantasy,* a thirty-minute, one-movement serial work commissioned by the Juilliard School of Music which premiered in a manner befitting its importance; it was the only work on the program and was performed twice with an intermission separating the two presentations. The audience, itself rather imposing, consisted of musicians, composers, and conductors from around the world.

Still another Copland work from this period was the orchestral suite *Music for a Great City,* commissioned by the London Symphony Orchestra and containing such segments as "Skyline," "Night Thoughts," and the cacophonous "Subway Jam." The piece premiered in London, where Copland conducted his favorite orchestra, the London Symphony, while Victor Kraft photographed the event. Versatile as ever, Copland subsequently wrote the signature theme for *CBS Playhouse,* a national television series.

The Tender Land

Perhaps the composer's most unique work during this period and one that merits special attention is his opera *The Tender Land,* a musical drama that some say reflected his sensibilities as a gay man living in conservative times. Commissioned by the League of Composers, the project was funded by Richard Rogers and Oscar Hammerstein and was originally envisioned as a television production. Because Copland agreed to compose the music, the League granted him permission to select the librettist, so he chose Erik Johns, his lover at the moment. Johns used the pseudonym Horace Everett so the public would not confuse his work as the creator of the opera's text with his activities as a dancer and artist.

The inspiration for Copland and Johns' scenario came from a 1939 book, *Let Us Now Praise Famous Men,* written by James Agee and illustrated by photographer Walker Evans. A stirring photo-essay of three tenant families struggling to survive in rural Alabama during the Great Depression, it sought to humanize the plight of the poor. In their subsequent opera, Copland and Johns retained the book's Great Depression time frame but shifted the setting to the rural Midwest.

In their story, a young woman, Laurie, is preparing to graduate from high school on the day that the story begins. She is at home with her mother, sister, and grandfather planning for the ceremony when the postman shows up and announces that two strangers, two men, have arrived in town. Before long, these strangers—the gentle Martin and the rambunctious Top—appear on the scene, and Top at once begins scheming to seduce the pretty young Laurie. His plan backfires, however, when Martin and Laurie meet, become infatuated, and resolve to go away together the next day. But, alas, something else happens instead: Martin and Top, after discussing the plan, decide it is they who will leave together and, indeed, they do so in the middle of the night. So it is that Laurie, discovering the next morning that the two men have departed without her, packs her bags and leaves as well, letting go of her family and turning her back on the forthcoming graduation ceremony; to be sure, an unorthodox ending given the era.

Not surprisingly, perhaps, the opera initially failed to find a buyer. Certainly network television would not touch it. After much finagling, however, the New York City Opera agreed to produce it with Jerome Robbins at the helm, but the gifted director simply could not make the production work. Consequently, *The Tender Land* opened to lackluster reviews and poor audience reception, prompting Johns to revise it substantially and ask Oberlin College to stage it the following year. The college did produce it, but as before, the reviews were tepid, as was the audience reaction.

One reason for the opera's failure stemmed from the fact that Copland had attempted to deal with turbulent moments in human life through the incongruent use of fresh, optimistic music not unlike that of *Appalachian Spring*. There was, however, an even more basic reason; the scenario depicted situations that made theatergoers uneasy, not the least being that its female lead relinquished her family ties and headed off alone toward an unknown future. In this respect, it has been suggested that the opera, particularly its conclusion, was actually a reflection of its creators' homosexuality, and that the story was essentially a coming-out tale, whether or not Copland and Johns intended it that way.

In an essay titled "Expanding Horizons: Sexuality and the Re-zoning of *The Tender Land*," Daniel Mathers ponders the opera's homosexual perspective.[46] He explains that its vantage point was that of the outsider, the gay person trapped in oppressive surroundings. Critic James McQuillen, while not addressing the homosexual subtext explicitly, concurs that the work was characterized by "ruefulness and the pain of isolation."[47] Of course, the fact that the two strangers in *The Tender Land*—the sensitive Martin and the intriguingly named Top—decide to steal away together during the night suggests they have a special bond, one that has no room for women. Furthermore, Laurie's decision to turn away from her family in a desperate effort to secure a better life for herself elsewhere is a common experience of the person who comes to realize that he or she is gay and leaves home in search of a freer, more authentic existence. Writes Mathers, "Laurie's 'coming out' is allegorical, taking her outside the confines of the picket fence, itself a type of social, cultural closet. She goes out into the world, which is seen as a refuge . . . separated from her enclosed upbringing."[48]

It should come as no surprise that Laurie, in the course of the opera, laments the fact that circumstances do not permit her to express her love openly. She sees no alternative but to escape from her surroundings and create a better future for herself in which she can love more forthrightly.

As could be expected, sheltered American audiences, particularly those that were not privy to Copland and Johns' homosexuality, were unable to recognize such implications in *The Tender Land*. For that matter, Copland and Johns, as mentioned earlier, may not have been entirely aware of these connotations themselves; certainly Copland has said had that his sexuality informed his work in an implicit fashion. Whatever the case, the opera has since come to be more widely respected, with certain contemporary critics regarding it as one of the finer American operas of the twentieth century. With the increased public awareness achieved in the ensuing decades through the advent of the feminist and gay rights movements, it makes sense that modern audiences would have a keener awareness and a better appreciation of the opera's nuanced meanings.

ELDER STATESMAN

After completing *The Tender Land,* Copland served as a guest conductor for several orchestras in the 1950s and 1960s for which he received mixed reviews from the musicians themselves. Although they enjoyed working with the legendary artist because he had a reputation for being good-humored and supportive during rehearsals, his talents as a conductor, similar to his gifts as a concert pianist, were not on a par with his compositional abilities. He was, first and foremost, a great composer.

During this period, Copland also spent a considerable amount of time at Tanglewood, the acclaimed music education center and summer home of the Boston Symphony Orchestra nestled away in the Berkshire Hills of Massachusetts. He had been involved with the institute since its inception, where he composed, performed, conducted, lectured, arranged concerts, and imported visiting composers from around the world. As well, he traveled the globe studying and critiquing the music of other nations.

At this time, he and his new lover, a dynamic young conductor named Robert Kennedy, visited Sweden, Finland, and Norway, where they acquainted themselves with modern Scandinavian compositions and met those who had created them. During their trip, the couple took in several other European nations as well, with Copland rekindling old friendships and forming new ones along the way.

Next came the Soviet Union. The State Department approached the composer as it had done in the past and asked him, once again, to represent the United States on a cultural tour overseas, this time to the USSR. Because his previous work for the government agency had met with hostile accusations from conspiracy-minded congressmen like Joseph McCarthy, Copland was understandably reluctant to comply with the request. Still, after weighing the proposal, he agreed to make the journey.

The composer toured the USSR for the next four weeks, during which time he took part in several concerts as a conductor and solo pianist. He also lectured at the Moscow Conservatory of Music and spoke on national radio. Most meaningful to him, however, were his meetings with the nation's younger generation of composers, none of whom had previously been permitted contact with Western composers and thus were in the dark about developments in their field outside the Soviet Union.

One of these composers was Arvo Pärt, at that time a twenty-five-year-old Estonian who supported himself by writing music for radio and television. Pärt's compositions tended toward the simple and the austere, and because of their religious themes, the otherworldly. Described today as a holy minimalist, his music shared several characteristics with that of Copland, including a distinctive purity.

A few years later, Copland visited the Soviet satellite nation Poland where he met, among others, composer Henryk Górecki. Similar to Copland, Górecki was drawn to folk music and folk text, which he sometimes integrated into his compositions, and he also favored an unadorned style and strove for emotional directness in his music. Described as a spiritual minimalist, Górecki eventually wrote the haunting *Symphony of Sorrowful Songs,* a work dedicated to the victims of

Auschwitz that incorporated into its text the prayer of an eighteen-year-old Jewish girl found scratched onto the wall of Gestapo headquarters in Zakopane, Poland. The doomed girl had etched the prayer for her mother.

Copland also toured Japan, where the progressive creations of Toru Takemitsu made a lasting impression on him. "I consider him to be one of the outstanding composers of our time," Copland later said.[49]

Takemitsu's music, which included his *Requiem for String Orchestra* written when he was only twenty-seven years old, became known for its use of silence and for its remarkable textures. Copland particularly appreciated the fact that Takemitsu seamlessly fused Eastern and Western styles, no easy task to be sure. In one respect, however, the two men differed: Takemitsu was receptive to novel forms of musical expression, most notably to the electronic music that was just coming into vogue, while Copland was more cautious. He felt that electronica lacked individuality and emotion—frankly, it bored him—but he left open the possibility that it might improve as it evolved, which indeed has proven to be the case.

Rock Hill Days

Back in the United States, meanwhile, lived another man who was also engaged in the debate about electronic music and who studiously composed it. His name was David Walker, and he was one of Copland's longtime friends as well as his part-time employee for over thirty years. Like Takemitsu, Walker was fascinated with the possibilities of electronic instrumentation, and dedicated his energies to creating it four days a week in his Greenwich Village flat. The remaining three days he spent at Copland's rambling, rustic home, where he served as the aging composer's personal secretary.

Copland's residence, known as Rock Hill, was situated in a heavily wooded area of Westchester County, New York, and was a simple, elegant structure trimmed in green. Although plain and unadorned, the house nevertheless possessed warmth and elegance. Victor Kraft, knowing the composer longed for a country home, came across Rock Hill while Copland was away on a concert tour of Europe. Upon his return, Copland fell in love with the property, in part because it contained a studio that overlooked the Hudson River in the distance.

Copland had always been a busy man who required help managing the myriad tasks that constituted his professional life, and this continued to be the case as he aged. Walker was the ideal person for the job, being a diligent, dignified, and self-directed man who shared many features with Copland himself. Perhaps for this reason the two remained on close personal terms until the composer's eventual demise. As for the possibility of a sexual element in their relationship, it appears that their attachment was strictly a platonic one. They were simply very good friends who worked well together.

Copland's romantic life had largely dried up by this point; he was now in his early seventies and no longer able to attract the young lovers he preferred. The handful of sexual attachments he did develop had occurred a few years earlier while he was still in his sixties and included two relationships with unstable young partners reminiscent of his past affair with the disturbed Victor Kraft. One was Robert Schiff, an alcoholic painter who required psychiatric hospitalization and eventually overdosed on a lethal mixture of drugs and alcohol. The other was a depressive whom the composer tried unsuccessfully to rehabilitate. By all accounts, Copland had always been moved by tortured young men whom he sought to rescue, a humane impulse that often failed to achieve the desired end. That said, not all of his relationships conformed to this pattern. He did enjoy a healthy relationship in his sixties with the well-adjusted twenty-seven-year-old Robert Cornell, the secretary of the New York City Ballet. It would be Copland's last serious affair.

In addition to facing an arid romantic life in his seventies, Copland more or less removed himself from events in the burgeoning gay community. He was put off by the militancy of the new breed of activists who had come to the fore following the Stonewall Riots of 1969. While he shared their belief in the need for equal rights for the gay and lesbian citizenry, he was uncomfortable with their confrontational tactics. Despite the composer's success, he had always been a modest man who shunned auspicious displays of power and position, instead favoring humility and self-restraint. It is therefore not surprising that he would prefer a more tempered approach to the public expression of one's sexuality, even when the issue extended into the political realm. Such a stance was consistent with the reserve he had displayed all his life, as well as being a common response among those of his generation.

This is not to imply, however, that Copland removed himself from all contact with other gay men—far from it. In his private life, he always surrounded himself with those who were gay or bisexual, often to the exclusion of women and heterosexual men. For this, he was sometimes criticized, even though his personal life was no one's concern but his own.

When in the company of his gay friends, Copland was known for being forthright about, as well as completely comfortable with, his and others' homosexuality. Be that as it may, he was still embarrassed by raucous displays of sexuality, gay or straight, even by those to whom he was close. One of his friends recalled the humorous way in which Copland would gasp and press his hand to the base of his neck when told a racy joke. He described it as Copland clutching his pearls.

Among the composer's gay friends were a large number of musicians, conductors, and fellow composers, among them Benjamin Britten, who was also his neighbor for a time. Another comrade was Leonard Bernstein, with whom Copland once had a brief affair. Despite his affection for Bernstein, Copland never appreciated the younger composer's efforts to conceal his own gayness. "Copland's homosexuality was less ambiguous than Bernstein's," writes Joan Peyser, "and for years Bernstein's connection to women, his quasi-romantic entanglements with them, irritated the older man, who called him— among friends—PH, for 'phony homosexual.'"[50] Still, Copland adored Bernstein even as he disapproved of Bernstein's sexual subterfuge, and the two ultimately enjoyed a lifelong association, personally as well as professionally.

In regard to Copland's professional life, by all accounts, he remained very active in the field of classical music as he grew older. Although he began suffering the first troubling signs of dementia in his early seventies—he developed problems with short-term memory— he continued conducting and lecturing. He largely gave up trying to compose, however, due to the memory impairment. More than anything else, Copland served as an ambassador of American music during this period, traveling the globe, introducing foreign audiences to American compositions, and conducting orchestras in such diverse locations as Hungary, Scotland, Czechoslovakia, Turkey, and El Salvador. In such venues, Copland's concerts featured selections from his own body of work, as well as those of Hindemith, Fauré, Mahler,

Tchaikovsky, and friend Benjamin Britten. Copland also continued to be involved in events at Tanglewood, where he led the Boston Symphony Orchestra from time to time. One thing he did not do, however, was accept a position as a full-time conductor. Because he still enjoyed a wide range of interests, he wished to retain a degree of flexibility in his commitments.

By this point, of course, it had become easy for the composer to travel abroad once again. He no longer encountered difficulty securing a passport or other documents. Domestic politics continued to intrude into his life. Copland still found himself confronted by thorny political matters on occasion, matters that sometimes began in the Oval Office itself.

A few years earlier President Lyndon Johnson had refused to invite him to the White House-sponsored Festival of the Arts because several renowned artists were planning to use the event to protest the Vietnam War and Johnson did not want anyone on the guest list who might be sympathetic to their cause. To determine who might constitute such a risky invitee, Johnson turned to McCarthy's list of suspected communists in the 1950s and made sure none of them were asked to attend. And this included Aaron Copland.

In other cases, the snub ran in the opposite direction. In 1973, President Richard Nixon contacted Copland, whose work he admired, and asked permission to use one of his compositions at the forthcoming presidential inauguration. Because Copland held the unscrupulous leader in very low regard, he was reluctant to grant the request. After giving the matter much thought, the composer did consent to the use of his music but refused to attend the ceremony. He did not want to be mistaken for a Nixon supporter. By comparison, Copland not only was present for the inauguration of President Jimmy Carter four years later, but he even conducted the Atlanta Symphony Orchestra during the ceremonies.

As it turns out, Carter's inauguration would be the last one in which Copland would participate. By the time he reached his early eighties, the composer was showing grave signs of dementia, the condition having progressed to the point that he was having difficulty recognizing old friends, as well as being highly distractible. Even in the face of such deterioration, however, he remained a gentle, kind man. The decline in his mental acuity could not extinguish the warmth and generosity he seemed to naturally exude.

Copland now spent his days at Rock Hill, where he and writer Vivian Perlis compiled his memoirs, two volumes' worth. Because the composer's memory had become so profoundly impaired, Perlis often had to obtain biographical material from transcripts of interviews he had given in years past; Copland simply could not recall such detailed information at will. When he was not working on these documents, he visited with the male and female admirers, mostly young musicians and artists, who came to Rock Hill to help care for the estate and bask in his presence. He was glad to have them in his home, since most of his peers had already died or were so uncomfortable seeing him in poor health that they stayed away. The upshot was that he found himself alone much of the time. Indeed, Perlis recalled how she and her husband visited Copland on his birthday, and to their dismay found that they were the only guests. Perhaps it was because of such isolation that he spent his later years engaged mainly in solitary activities, such as listening to the music of Igor Stravinsky or reading the works of André Gide, although even the latter inevitably came to an end due to dementia. Sadly, Copland reached the point where he could no longer comprehend even a newspaper article. Around-the-clock nursing care was required by this juncture, although he never lost the capacity to enjoy the music he had always loved.

Finally, on December 2, 1990, Copland passed away at Phelps Memorial Hospital in Tarrytown, New York. The cause of death was respiratory failure due to pneumonia. He was ninety years old.

After his demise, Copland's body was cremated and his ashes buried at Tanglewood, the interment being accompanied by a spare, secular ceremony as he had requested. In his will, he bequeathed a portion of his wealth to the creation of the Aaron Copland Fund for Composers, today known as the Aaron Copland Fund for Music, which grants nearly a half-million dollars a year to performing groups in need of financial support. In a previous will, he had also left money to Victor Kraft and Harold Clurman, but since both men preceded him in death, he had revised the document. As well, his instructions stipulated that part of his estate be channeled into the Nadia Boulanger Memorial Foundation, among other worthy causes.

THE COPLAND LEGACY

In the twenty-first century, we remember Aaron Copland as the creator of innovative musical works boasting a uniquely American sound. Among his nearly 100 compositions were symphonies, operas, ballets, and choral works for concert stage, radio, television, and film. He also wrote books for the general public, including *Copland on Music, Music and Imagination,* and *What to Listen for in Music.* In addition, he scripted and hosted a twelve-part series, *Music in the 20s,* for National Educational Television, and took part in a documentary about his own life, *Aaron Copland: A Self-Portrait,* that aired on the Public Broadcasting Service in 1985.

Copland was the recipient of more than thirty honorary degrees from such prestigious universities as Harvard, Brandeis, Brown, Oberlin, and Princeton. Institutions were also named in his honor, among them the Aaron Copland School of Music at Queens College in New York City. In addition, he received high praise from the White House: President Kennedy awarded him the Medal for Distinguished Service, President Johnson presented him with the Presidential Medal of Freedom, and President Reagan honored him with the Medal of the Arts. Even the House of Representatives got into the act, awarding him the Congressional Gold Medal, the highest honor Congress can bestow upon a citizen. These citations were in addition to his Pulitzer Prize and Academy Award.

Of course, such accolades mean little or nothing if the artist on whom they are conferred is forgotten over the course of time. In the case of Copland, however, this has not happened. His name has retained its luster through the years and commands respect even today, in an era pervaded by the cult of celebrity, one overrun by those avidly seeking attention and fame. This should not be all that surprising given that Copland's renown has always been based on genuine talent. Music scholars have long hailed him as the most gifted American composer to ever have lived, with some admirers, such as Igor Stravinsky, insisting that Copland should be praised not merely as a great American composer but as one of the world's great composers.

Copland's remarkable canon of works have become a mainstay of the repertories of countless orchestras, both domestic and foreign, and have inspired artists in associated fields. It is surely no overstatement to say that his achievements continue to resonate around the world. What is perhaps most striking, though, is that he accomplished so much in spite of being a gay, Jewish man living in a century when neither his sexual orientation nor his religious background was held in high esteem by the majority of the population. Nevertheless, through his extraordinary musical genius, diplomatic demeanor, and boundless spirit of kindness and generosity, Copland succeeded in surmounting the discrimination to which he was subjected while displaying the heights that may be scaled by the person who is dedicated to the artistic expression of the beauty of human life.

NOTES

1. Anonymous, *Aaron Copland: Biography.* Sony Web site <www.sonyclassical. com/artists/copland/bio.html>, p. 1.

2. In Varnell, Paul, *Aaron Copland at 100.* Independent Gay Forum Web site <www.indegayforum.org/articles/varnell42.html>, p. 2.

3. Aaron Copland, in Copland, Aaron and Perlis, Vivian, *Copland: 1900 Through 1942* (New York: St. Martin's/Griffin, 1984, p. 18).

4. Ibid.

5. Aaron Copland, in Pollack, Howard, *Aaron Copland: The Life and Work of an Uncommon Man* (New York: Henry Holt, 1999, p. 24).

6. Copland, Aaron, Letter to Parents (September 14, 1921; New York: Aaron Copland Fund for Music). Library of Congress, *American Memory* Web site <http://memory.loc.gov/ammem/achtml/achome.html>, p. 1.

7. Clurman, in Copland and Perlis, *Copland: 1900 Through 1942,* p. 57.

8. Ibid.

9. Boulanger, in Jones, Quincy, *Q: The Autobiography of Quincy Jones* (New York: Doubleday, 2001, p. 133).

10. Schonberg, Harold, *The Lives of Great Composers,* Third Edition (New York: W. W. Norton, 1997, p. 481).

11. Aaron Copland, in Levin, Gail and Tick, Judith, *Aaron Copland's America: A Cultural Perspective* (New York: Watson-Guptill Publications, 2000, p. 136).

12. Levin and Tick, *Aaron Copland's America,* pp. 135-136.

13. Copland, Aaron, *Music and Imagination* (Cambridge, MA: Harvard University Press, 1980, pp. 99-100).

14. Jones, *Q,* p. 322.

15. Tommasini, Anthony, *Virgil Thomson: Composer on the Aisle* (New York: W. W. Norton, 1997, p. 180).

16. Bernstein, in Tommasini, *Virgil Thomson,* p. 563.

17. Peyser, Joan, *The Memory of All That: The Life of George Gershwin* (New York: Simon and Schuster, 1993, pp. 98-99).

18. Rockwell, John, *Copland, Dean of American Music, dies at ninety* (December 3, 1990). *The New York Times on the Web* <nytimes.com/books/99/03/14/specials/copland-obit.html>, p. 2.

19. Greenberg, Rodney, *George Gershwin* (London: Phaidon Press, 1998, p. 135)

20. Aaron Copland, in Dickinson, Peter, ed., *Copland Connotations: Studies and Interviews* (Woodbridge, England: Boydell Press, 2002, p. 67).

21. Aaron Copland, in Greenberg, *George Gershwin,* p. 135.

22. Copland (1984, p. 130).

23. Greenberg, *George Gershwin,* p. 135.

24. Aaron Copland, in Schonberg, *The Lives of Great Composers,* p. 564.

25. Rockwell, *Copland,* p. 1.

26. Aaron Copland, in Tommasini, *Virgil Thomson,* p. 292.

27. Perlis, in Copland, Aaron and Perlis, Vivian, *Copland: After 1943* (New York: St. Martin's/Griffin, 1989, p. 309).

28. Ibid., p. 401.

29. Schonberg, *The Lives of Great Composers,* p. 564.

30. Aaron Copland, in Schonberg, *The Lives of Great Composers,* p. 565.

31. Ibid.

32. Levin and Tick, *Aaron Copland's America,* p. 47.

33. Lee, in Dickinson, *Copland Connotations,* p. 104.

34. Graham, in Dickinson, *Copland Connotations,* p. 107.

35. Copland, in Copland and Perlis, *Copland: After 1943,* p. 33.

36. Copland, Aaron, *What Copland Says: 10 Quotes from the Composer. MPR* Web site <music.mpr.org/features/ 0011_copland/quotes_by.shtml>, p. 2.

37. Johns, in Dickinson, *Copland Connotations,* p. 123.

38. Copland, in Varnell, *Aaron Copland at 100,* p. 3.

39. Thomson, in Tommasini, *Virgil Thomson,* p. 301.

40. Cage, in Tommasini, *Virgil Thomson,* p. 443.

41. Forster, in Navasky, Victor, *Naming Names* (New York: Penguin Books, 1980, 1991, p. 112).

42. McCarthy, in Copland and Perlis, *Copland: After 1943,* p. 192.

43. Aaron Copland, in CNN report (May 5, 2003), *Senate Unseals McCarthy Transcripts.* CNN Web site <cnn.com/2003/ALLPOLITICS/05/05/mccarthy.hearings/ index.html>, p. 1.

44. Aaron Copland, in Copland and Perlis, *Copland: After 1943,* p. 193.

45. Aaron Copland, in Schiff, Who Was That Masked Composer? (January 2000). *The Atlantic Monthly Online* Web site <www.theatlantic.com/issues/2000/ 01/001schiff.htm>, p. 5.

46. Mathers, in Dickinson, *Copland Connotations.*

47. McQuillen, James, Try a Little Tenderness (review) (April 21, 1999). Willamette Week Web site <www.wweek.com/html/perfa042199.html>, p. 3.

48. Mathers, in Dickinson, *Copland Connotations,* p. 133.

49. Gould, Glenn, *Toru Takemitsu: A Profile.* Glenn Gould/Sony Web site <www. glenngould.com/gg/toru.html>, p. 1.

50. Peyser, Joan, *Bernstein: A Biography* (New York: William Morrow/Beach Tree Books, 1987, pp. 53-54).

REFERENCES

Anonymous (2002). *Aaron Copland: Biography.* Sony Web site <www.sonyclassical. com/artists/copland/bio.html>.

Anonymous (2003). Senate unseals McCarthy transcripts. CNN Web site <www. cnn.com/2003/ALLPOLITICS/05/05/mccarthy.hearings/index.html>.

Copland, Aaron (1921). Letter to parents. New York: Aaron Copland Fund for Music. Library of Congress, *American Memory* Web site <http://memory.loc.gov/ammem/achtml/achome.html>.

Copland, Aaron (1980). *Music and Imagination.* Cambridge, MA: Harvard University Press.

Copland, Aaron (2002). *What Copland Says: 10 Quotes from the Composer. MPR* Web site <music.mpr.org/features/0011 _copland/quotes_by.shtml>.

Copland, Aaron and Perlis, Vivian (1984). *Copland: 1900 Through 1942.* New York: St. Martin's/Griffin.

Copland, Aaron and Perlis, Vivian (1989). *Copland: After 1943.* New York: St. Martin's/Griffin.

Dickinson, Peter (Ed.) (2002). *Copland Connotations: Studies and Interviews.* Woodbridge, England: Boydell Press.

Gould, Glenn (2000). *Toru Takemitsu: A Profile.* Glenn Gould/Sony Web site <www.glenngould.com/gg/toru.html>.

Greenberg, Rodney (1998). *George Gershwin.* London: Phaidon Press.

Jones, Quincy (2001). *Q: The Autobiography of Quincy Jones.* New York: Doubleday.

Levin, Gail and Tick, Judith (2000). *Aaron Copland's America: A Cultural Perspective.* New York: Watson-Guptill Publications.

McQuillen, James (1999). Try a Little Tenderness (review). Willamette Week Web site <www.wweek.com/html/perfa042199.html>.

Navasky, Victor (1980, 1991). *Naming Names.* New York: Penguin Books.

Peyser, Joan (1987). *Bernstein: A Biography.* New York: William Morrow/Beach Tree Books.

Peyser, Joan (1993). *The Memory of All That: The Life of George Gershwin.* New York: Simon and Schuster.

Pollack, Howard (1999). *Aaron Copland: The Life and Work of an Uncommon Man.* New York: Henry Holt.

Rockwell, John (1990). *Copland, Dean of American Music, dies at ninety. The New York Times on the Web* <www.nytimes.com/books/99/03/14/specials/copland-obit.html>.

Schiff, David (2000). Who was that masked composer? *The Atlantic Monthly Online* Web site <www.theatlantic.com/issues/2000/01/001schiff.htm>.

Schonberg, Harold (1997). *The Lives of Great Composers,* Third Edition. New York: W. W. Norton.

Tommasini, Anthony (1997). *Virgil Thomson: Composer on the Aisle.* New York: W. W. Norton.

Varnell, Paul (2002). Aaron Copland at 100. *Independent Gay Forum* Web site <www.indegayforum.org/articles/varnell42.html>.

DAG HAMMARSKJÖLD

UN Secretary-General Dag Hammarskjöld at a press conference held at United Nations Headquarters, March 24, 1960. (UN/DPI Photo.)

INTRODUCTION

On a warm September night in 1961, a middle-aged gentleman, blond and slender, stood waiting to board a private jet at a small, worn airport in Léopoldville, capital of the fledgling Republic of the Congo. His name was Dag Hammarskjöld, and he was the Secretary-General of the United Nations. Twice elected to the post by unanimous votes of the General Assembly, he was one of the most respected and influential figures in world politics. His mission in Africa was to try to convince a militant breakaway faction to stop firing on UN peacekeeping forces who had been stationed in the region. On this autumn evening, however, the distinguished Swede found himself experiencing more than the usual amount of trepidation associated with such a mission, in part because he was about to board an aircraft that, only hours earlier, had been fired upon while flying over the Congo. An ominous turn of events, the incident had troubled Hammarskjöld deeply. Bystanders at the airport later described the look of worry on his face and recalled how, from time to time, he approached the handful of men and women in his delegation and spoke to them in hushed tones before returning his gaze to the plane that sat waiting for them on the runway.

As it turned out, he had reason to worry. At sunrise the next morning, villagers in the bush spoke of the great flash they had seen in the night sky, a burst of light so bright that it had illuminated the heavens. Congolese officials, meanwhile, notified the Secretary-General's staff at United Nations headquarters in Manhattan that Hammarskjöld's plane had failed to arrive in Ndola and was being classified as missing. Without delay, the global organization issued a call for help in locating it, and the request was promptly honored. Several embassies in Central Africa dispatched search planes, which, together with reconnaissance aircraft furnished by the Congolese government, scanned the jungles throughout the morning and afternoon hours. Finally, a pilot detected what appeared to be charred foliage and the remains of an airplane nine miles outside Ndola. The search then moved to the ground.

Hacking their way though the vegetation, a team of rescue workers arrived at the wreckage at sundown. There they found fragments of scorched metal and fourteen bodies burned beyond recognition. Rather astonishingly, the team also came upon a corpse that was fully recognizable, the face "a mask of repose and serenity," in the words of writer Israel Levine.[1] It was Dag Hammarskjöld.

Continuing to comb through the debris, rescuers discovered a remaining victim, a UN security guard, who was badly burned but clinging to life. Though dazed, he used his last breaths to recount the final moments of the flight. According to his report, as well as those of witnesses in the bush, it appears that terrorists may have brought down the plane, terrorists who opposed Hammarskjöld's peacekeeping efforts in the troubled region.

In the days that followed, millions of people around the world mourned the fallen statesman, with dignitaries from scores of nations paying formal tribute to him. Although the public was both aware and respectful of Hammarskjöld's historic accomplishments, as well as deeply saddened by his tragic death, most people knew little about Dag Hammarskjöld, the man. Those who did were not talking, opting instead to respect his privacy even in death. Abetting their efforts were subsequent biographers, virtually all of whom, in the years following his demise, sought to present the former Secretary-General in nearly mythical terms, obscuring or blatantly denying those personal features that did not correspond to the conventional image of a hero, even when such features were integral to his being.

Still, in the decades since his tragic death, much has come to light about the statesman. Today it is often assumed that he was homosexual, although perhaps abstinent. It is also known that he was a profoundly spiritual man who felt tormented at times, even suicidal, a man who harbored dark doubts about the future of the human race. For that matter, he seems to have suffered doubts about his own future, convinced, throughout his adult years, that he was destined to die in a moment of self-sacrifice.

To better understand and appreciate Dag Hammarskjöld this biographical account will revisit the people and circumstances that helped set the trajectory of his remarkable career, as well as recount the rather astonishing events of his life itself. This biographical sketch begins by exploring his childhood in an aristocratic family, a family presided over by his father, the Prime Minister of Sweden, and his mother, a humanitarian and lover of the arts. Persuasive parents, they helped shape his beliefs, his values, and ultimately his deeds on behalf of the world community. By becoming acquainted with these and other salient features of Hammarskjöld's existence, and by distinguishing the facts from the distortions of prior biographers, readers will come to know, more accurately and more intimately, this exceptional man, one of the twentieth century's most principled and influential figures.

THE RED CASTLE

Dag Hammarskjöld was born July 29, 1905, with the proverbial silver spoon in his mouth. The fourth son of Hjalmar and Agnes Hammarskjöld, his family lived in an imposing red castle on a hill overlooking the rooftops and spires of the ancient Swedish city of Uppsala. Such impressive circumstances were not new to the Hammarskjölds. Long revered in their homeland, they could trace their lineage back to the seventeenth century, when the king knighted a cavalry officer for his valiant services to the crown and bestowed upon him the Hammarskjöld surname, which means "hammer and shield."

His doting mother lavished affection on him in his early years that was unusual in both manner and degree. Having already borne three sons—Bo, Åke, and Sten—she became pregnant with Dag when she was in her forties, and knowing this would be her last child, yearned for a daughter. When she delivered yet another boy, Agnes was delighted nonetheless, although she soon began fashioning his appearance into that of a girl. She allowed his silky blond hair to fall in ringlets to his shoulders so that it framed his angelic face, a look so striking that her friends called him "Goldilocks."[2] She also dressed him in blouses, ruffled skirts, and bonnets to heighten his feminine appearance.

Addressing this rather odd practice, previous Hammarskjöld biographers sought to downplay its importance. A few even defended the custom.

"Some have suggested that his mother's . . . habit of dressing him in lace-trimmed skirts and letting his locks grow long had a bearing on Dag's future sexual interests," writes Emery Kelen. "I am not impressed with this opinion. Oscar Wilde was not the only person who wore skirts and locks when he was young; Franklin Delano Roosevelt did too, and so did Winston Churchill."[3]

Journalist Burnet Hershey maintained that the practice was merely a curious convention of the era. Describing it as an "optional custom," he explained that it was not unheard-of among Europeans of that day and age.[4]

In fact, both writers are correct. At the beginning of the twentieth century, a minority of parents did indeed clothe their young sons in garments of the opposite sex, with no apparent effect on the boys' sexual development. In the case of Dag Hammarskjöld, however, two facts stand out that previous biographers seem to have sidestepped. First, Agnes does not appear to have dressed her other sons in girls' attire when they were youngsters, only Dag. Second, her husband Hjalmar opposed the practice, even insisting that Dag's hair be cut and boys' clothing worn when he began attending kindergarten. Hjalmar, a member of the prestigious Nobel Committee and a high government official, wished for his son to fit in with the other school-children. The fact is, Agnes encouraged Dag's femininity because she regarded him as the daughter she had long desired. Once, she even told a group of friends, "You know, [Hjalmar] and I have always been very sorry we never had a daughter—but Dag has been just like a daughter to us."[5]

Certainly it is true that Dag, as a youngster, spent most of his time with his mother, being very much a part of her social and religious life. When her friends came to visit, he helped her serve tea, and each Sunday, without fail, accompanied her to church. He shared, too, in her humanitarian work. A devout Lutheran, Agnes was a firm believer in Christian charity, and for this reason often traveled with Dag in tow to the outskirts of the city, where together they ministered to the poor. By all accounts, he was powerfully drawn to his mother, as were most people who knew her.

Described, rather quaintly, as "a feminine person of plump tendencies," Agnes wore her hair arranged high on her head—very stylish at the time—and moved with a sense of grace and self-possession.[6] Brimming with warmth and kindness, she was generous, charming, gregarious, and good-humored. Indeed, this was a woman who gave herself so fully to laughter that those around her sometimes thought she was crying, so spectacular was her bellowing. Acquaintances also spoke of her sympathy for the destitute and dispossessed, as well as her wide-ranging aesthetic and intellectual pursuits, interests she made it a point to pass on to Dag.

Although Agnes undoubtedly possessed fine qualities that helped her son develop into a conscientious and humane statesman, her larger-than-life presence may also have overwhelmed him and interfered with his emotional development. Even the most apologetic Hammarskjöld biographers have acknowledged that she was the centerpiece of Dag's early existence, a figure to whom he was totally devoted. Less often, they have conceded that he was utterly dependent on her as well.

As for the reasons behind this intense mother-son bond, several explanations have been offered over the years that go beyond the fact that Agnes was an overly solicitous woman who longed for a daughter. Some have said the attachment was related to Dag's own feminine nature and needs, while others have claimed it was the result of his father's frequent absences from home.

It has been suggested that Dag's "tender disposition" caused him to relate instinctively to women and their pursuits.[7] Supporters of this explanation claim that as a boy he was emotionally sensitive and for this reason was drawn to women, especially to his mother and her friends, as well as to their pastimes.

In terms of the latter explanation—the "absent father" hypothesis—those who hold to this notion point out that Hjalmar's career often required him to be away from home for long stretches of time, thereby causing Dag to lack a father figure. Appointed Ambassador to Denmark shortly after Dag was born, the senior Hammarskjöld held the post for two years, during which time his contact with his family was limited. He subsequently petitioned the king for a job that would return him to his homeland, and the monarch responded by naming him Governor of Uppland Province, then Prime Minister of Sweden, a position in which Hjalmar was second in power to the king himself.

Serving as Prime Minister, however, did not bring him any closer to his family. Hjalmar spent nearly all of his time in Stockholm, paying visits to his wife and sons in Uppsala, forty miles away, on weekends. For this reason, Agnes, whose three older sons were now well into adolescence or approaching adulthood, fixed her attention on young Dag, the adoration she ladled on him perhaps being a way for her to meet some of her unfulfilled needs as a wife and mother. In much the same way, Dag seems to have looked to Agnes for the affection he was not receiving from his father and brothers. "Out of sheer necessity," writes Levine, "he turned to his mother for the companionship he could not find elsewhere."[8]

Still, the situation was not all that dire. Although Hjalmar was seldom at home, Dag did have prospective companions around him every day. Furthermore, when Hjalmar was at the castle, he was not a particularly attentive father, being preoccupied with affairs of state much of the time. Even when his thoughts were not on political issues, he was emotionally unavailable to his family.

Those who knew him have said that unlike his affectionate and effusive wife, Hjalmar was rarely warm or demonstrative. A tall, bald man with a goatee, a monocle, and a cane, he was widely regarded as arrogant, autocratic, and glacial, a man so aloof that he was once described as a "block of granite."[9] Known for alienating many colleagues who otherwise admired his professional skills, some have said he harbored an outright contempt for humanity. All the same, he did command respect. An expert in international law, Hjalmar was instrumental in constructing Sweden's political strategies during World War I. He also was a member in good standing of the nation's social elite, being on cordial terms with several Nobel laureates, not to mention the King and Queen of Sweden, who were known for dropping by the castle for dinner when Hjalmar was in residence.

To Dag, however, Hjalmar was not a political and social luminary. He was simply his father, and an overbearing one at that. "I myself stand in the center of a perpetual conflict with a dominating father, whose pressure I hated and whose weaknesses I always saw very clearly," Dag told a friend many years later.[10] It may well have been the case, then, that he did not exactly yearn for his father's company.

Dag did enjoy the presence of Agnes and the children in his neighborhood, most notably Jon and Yvonne Söderblom, the son and daughter of the Archbishop of Uppsala who lived in a palace down the hill from the Hammarskjölds. These children often visited Dag at the castle, where they spent many hours absorbed in adventure, the edifice being a veritable dreamworld for the youngsters.

The castle was one of the oldest structures in Sweden, known as the "red castle" because of its reddish-brown hue. The ruthless King Gustavus Vasa ordered the castle to be built in 1523. Originally intended as a fortress, the compound was used during its first three centuries as a palace for the kingdom's rulers, many of whom were truly intimidating. Among its formidable occupants was Gustavus' great-granddaughter Christina, who as a lesbian and heir to the throne, demanded she be crowned king, not queen, of Sweden. The castle's appearance reflected the character of its steely inhabitants, being a daunting structure distinguished by battlements and turrets. Because of its bleak appearance Agnes Hammarskjöld set out to transform it into a gracious family dwelling during her term at the estate, closing off many of its stark, cavernous rooms and turning the interior space of a tower into a circular banquet room. She also converted the great Hall of State into a magnificent playroom for her children that became a favorite spot for Dag, yet this was not his only recreational area.

From his bedroom window, he could look down upon the spires of Uppsala's ancient Lutheran cathedral and the countryside that lay beyond the city's edge. With the Sönderblom children, he explored the secret passages that lay hidden inside the castle's massive walls and played hide-and-seek in its underground hallways, corridors that led to murky dungeons. During the glistening Swedish winters, he and his friends sledded down the hill to the Palace of the Archbishop. To be sure, Dag's surroundings were magical, as were his family's holiday celebrations, events the Hammarskjölds observed on a scale befitting an aristocratic household.

On Christmas Eve, Agnes and the servants would prepare a feast for family and friends in the ornate dining hall, a banquet consisting of ham, fish, and an enormous cheese round, the annual gift from the Swedish dairy association. All manner of sweets would also be doled out, after which the guests would gather around the Christmas tree shimmering with candlelight, sing carols, and listen as Agnes read from the Bible.

Of course, Dag loved the yuletide season, as could be expected given his age. It was his favorite time of year partly because it allowed him a brief respite from his schoolwork, although he did not dislike academic activities. He enjoyed studying, and was among the brightest and most self-disciplined students in the public elementary school he attended. Dag's interests were quite diverse, a characteristic he likely acquired from his mother. Among other subjects, he was drawn to music, art, literature, science, and history, spending much of his time absorbed in books, to some extent because he had so few friends among his classmates.

Those who attended grade school with him have said that Dag did not relate well to others. One classmate in particular, a colonel's son named Jarl, recalled that the youngest Hammarskjöld exuded "an indefinable don't-touch-me air that kept you at your distance."[11]

Certainly it is possible that Dag's aloofness stemmed from the fact that he was the Prime Minister's son, and as such was inclined to look down his nose at his peers in the public school. Such haughtiness could almost be predicted. Other explanations are equally plausible, though, one of which concerns his surroundings.

At home and quite innocently, it is conceivable that he acquired a superficially snobbish manner, a personal style mirroring the imperious behavior of those at the castle. If so, then his cool comportment was not so much an expression of genuine conceit as a reflection of his background in an aristocratic milieu. Supporting this notion is the fact that to many observers Dag appeared far from arrogant, even shy and uncertain at times, his outward demeanor being at odds with the boy himself.

It is feasible, too, that his standoffish manner was a cautious, self-protective stance erected in response to the negative opinions of others. By all accounts, he had reason to feel defensive. Among other affronts, Dag had to endure his classmates' hostile comments about his famous yet controversial father, cutting remarks the children no doubt heard voiced in their own homes. As well, he had to contend with taunts directed at himself, which perhaps is not surprising given that he was a frail, passive child who was visibly uncomfortable with the roughhouse antics of other boys. Indeed, Dag was considered his school's peacemaker because he stringently avoided fistfights and discouraged schoolyard disputes among others. He also immersed himself in books rather than playing team sports and chose to spend his free time with his mother instead of his schoolmates, preferences that did little to endear him to the other students.

It may have been the case, then, that Dag, feeling different from and occasionally rebuffed by his classmates, constructed a wall around himself when he was in their presence. This barrier insulated him from their criticism while he remained near his mother whenever circumstances permitted. In the same vein, he may have plunged into books partly to escape from painful social situations. In this way emotionally vulnerable children, including gay children, often cope with adverse conditions at home or school.

But even as he lacked social acumen, Dag was rapidly acquiring another type of knowledge that would serve him well in later life, namely, political knowledge. When he was only nine years old, he developed a consuming interest in political science, one fueled by the discussions he and his older brothers had begun having with their father when Hjalmar returned from Stockholm for weekend visits. It was also an interest kindled by the times, this being the eve of World War I.

As Prime Minister, Hjalmar was in an ideal position to bring to his family new and disturbing reports of the impending battle, troubling updates he provided at the dinner table. Afterward, the family would sit for hours debating the possible Swedish approaches to the conflict. Years later Dag recalled that it was these talks more than anything else that had brought about his own political awakening.

Among the lessons he learned during this time, Dag came to understand the process of military escalation, that is, the way in which a small-scale disagreement may snowball overnight into a large-scale bloodbath. He also came to discern the high cost of refusing to participate in such madness, a truth he grasped by observing firsthand his father's stormy tenure as Prime Minister during the war years.

Hjalmar, early in the dispute, decided to maintain the traditional Swedish position of noninvolvement, and struggled night and day to keep his nation out of the fray. Certainly it was true that Sweden, during the preceding 100 years, had rigorously pursued a hands-off policy in other nations' feuds, so Hjalmar's stance was consistent with the historical record. His allusion to tradition was also an astute diplomatic move in that it concealed his personal views of the war. On his weekend visits to the castle Hjalmar shared his thoughts with his family. His opinion of the war was the same as that of most other Swedes of the day, namely, that it was a conflict that concerned Sweden not a whit but only invited trouble for the Scandinavian nation. This view was not a particularly surprising one, given that the Swedish people had long considered armed conflict to be a primitive means of settling disagreements. To them, "power politics" was crass and the "might makes right" mentality, barbaric. With the advent of World War I, their opinion seemed particularly well-founded.

This Swedish viewpoint soon came to be embraced by a growing number of people in surrounding nations, most notably in England, which endured enormous losses in the early months of the conflict. As Paul Fussell writes in *The Great War and Modern Memory,* "Casualties had been shocking, positions had settled into self-destructive stalemate, and sensitive people now perceived that the war, far from promising to be 'over by Christmas,' was going to extend itself to hitherto unimagined reaches of suffering and irony."[12] Yet despite the war's dispiriting character and course, there remained a number of pro-war diehards, including those in Sweden, who cheered it on while criticizing Hjalmar's policy of neutrality, calling it cowardly. Although their castigation rankled the Prime Minister, he held his ground.

Unfortunately, such animosity was also directed at Dag on occasion, most often at school, where his fellow students chided him because his father refused to enlist their nation in the war. At one point, rather ironically, Dag was even drawn into a scuffle because of his father's pacifistic stance, an altercation which Dag wrote a poem about years later. Of course, such incidents did little to boost his flagging self-esteem, but they did cause him to seriously re-examine his father's neutralist position.

In further talks with Hjalmar, he listened as his father outlined the pragmatic aspects of noninvolvement. Hjalmar pointed out that the Swedish government, by remaining an objective third party, might someday be in a position to help negotiate a settlement to the war. Even if this did not prove to be the case, Hjalmar explained that he and his government could still help construct a more stable Europe afterward. Thus, he maintained that Sweden, by refusing to take sides, was situating itself to provide critical diplomacy that eventually could produce a better world. Dag, perhaps instinctively, understood and respected his father's strategy. After all, Dag had already established himself as his school's playground mediator; conciliation was apparently in his blood.

The war concluded on November 11, 1918. In all, sixty-five million military personnel had been involved in the fight worldwide, eight million of whom perished in the trenches or at sea. Another seven million civilians died as well. Other penalties included a ravaged European economy and a deadly outbreak of influenza, an illness spread across the globe by troops returning to their homelands.

Most consequential, though, the conflict laid the groundwork for World War II, although this was not immediately evident.

The war years took quite a toll on Dag, largely because he was forced to endure the searing public hatred of his father. He encountered this enmity not only at school, but also on the streets of Uppsala and in the nation's newspapers. Nevertheless, he admired his father's determination to remain true to his convictions in the face of rampant scorn. In later life, he even used Hjalmar's unswerving commitment to his principles as a model for his own conduct. Similar to his mother Agnes, however, Dag also strove to be aware and considerate of the opinions of others, and struggled to express himself honestly and tactfully. As well, he availed himself of new ideas, his curious mind welcoming such challenges. Dag now understood how a local dispute could spin out of control and lead to global slaughter. In such ways, his childhood experiences of wartime life etched an indelible impression on his perceptive young mind and instilled in him the desire to dedicate himself to a life of public service.

GOLDEN BOY

Sweden, like most other European nations, approached the years following World War I in a spirit of hope, clinging naively to the belief that never again would a conflict emerge as devastating as the one that had just gripped the continent. Dag shared this sunny optimism, even though he was only in his mid-teens and vastly inexperienced in the ways of the world. Despite his innocence he possessed far more political knowledge than other Swedish youths, due mainly to the in-depth talks he continued having with his father.

Young Hammarskjöld remained a bit standoffish as an adolescent, and unlike other boys, showed neither a curiosity about, nor an attraction to, girls. He steadfastly refused to date, even staying at home rather than attending his school's annual dances. This was despite the fact that social gatherings of this type were customary highlights of the Swedish school year, with pressure being brought to bear on all students—above all, on the Governor's son—to be present. But Hammarskjöld showed no interest in girls and considered dances a waste of time. And that was that. He did take pleasure in skiing and other winter sports, activities he enjoyed alone or in the company of other boys.

Hammarskjöld's overarching interest during his adolescent years was world affairs, a fascination that was no doubt authentic. Yet there may have been another reason for his attraction to a subject matter that was, by its nature, far removed from his immediate existence: by losing himself in such a distant, impersonal field as international politics, he could avoid any thorny parental or sexual conflicts that might otherwise arise. Certainly, such issues are common features of adolescence, particularly among those who are gay, although not all youths tackle them at this time. Some postpone them for years or evade them throughout their lifetimes. Hammarskjöld appears to have been one of these avoidant sorts, his teenage immersion in foreign affairs being part genuine interest, part defense mechanism. Although this formula was initially effective in stimulating his intellect while keeping personal conflicts at bay, the strategy eventually caused him immense frustration. All the same, he continued to submerge himself in the subject of global politics while carefully sidestepping more personal matters, particularly sexual ones, throughout his teens.

Hammarskjöld was drawn to the prospect of a worldwide peacekeeping entity and followed closely the creation of the League of Nations. This occurred at the end of World War I, when political leaders around the globe, appalled by the horror and waste they had just witnessed, set out to ensure that violence on such a massive scale would never again be unleashed.

In a timely essay, titled "The Idea of a League of Nations," H. G. Wells wrote, "All the world has come to look upon (war) as a sort of mythological monster, which, if left to itself, will periodically re-emerge from hell, to devour the whole youth and the whole wealth of civilized mankind."[13] To preempt such a monster, an organization known as the League of Nations was born January 10, 1919, in Geneva, Switzerland, with the leaders of Britain, Italy, France, and the United States—the "Big Four"—convening in Paris a week later to draft its covenant.

A pioneering federation, the League had a trio of ambitious aims: to bring about worldwide disarmament, to protect the sovereignties and rights of its member nations, and to settle disputes between countries before they escalated to armed conflict. As it turned out, the

League and its covenant would soon become the focus of marked attention in capitals around the world, as well as in the Hammarskjöld household.

As most everyone else in Sweden, Dag had high hopes for the organization's ability to avert future battles. World War I had certainly proven the need for such a body. His father, however, while agreeing in principle that a multinational peacekeeping alliance was desirable, harbored great skepticism about the League's chances for success, even questioning whether it would get off the ground at all. This was particularly the case after the United States announced its refusal to participate.

Such problems notwithstanding, sixty-three nations joined the League during its formative years, ranging from former central powers such as Germany, Austria, and Hungary, to emerging world powers, most notably China and Russia, to neutral countries such as Sweden and Switzerland. In terms of the United States' refusal to take part, it was universally denounced as a betrayal of world peace. Nevertheless, young Hammarskjöld held firm to his belief that the coalition could serve a valuable function even in the absence of American participation, while his father, although remaining doubtful of the League's prospects, agreed to serve as a delegate to the organization's Disarmament Conference. Dag took enormous pride in this.

He also took pride in his studies, becoming one of the top students in his high school class. His final report card consisted of eight As and one B, the latter in physical education; he had never been the athletic type. Despite his outstanding academic performance, however, Hjalmar felt compelled to compare Dag's grade card to that of his older brothers.

"Åke's was better," Hjalmar told him dismissively.[14]

Taking this not-so-subtle criticism in stride, Hammarskjöld, at the age of seventeen, entered Uppsala University. By now he had grown into a tall young man with a rosy complexion and sea-blue eyes. Described as handsome "in a gentle sort of way," his facial expression was typically open and receptive, his eyes seldom blinking.[15]

He decided to seek a degree in the humanities on the advice of his parents. His major concentrations centered on the history of literature, political economy, philosophy, and French. He also studied Portuguese, Spanish, and classical Greek, having already attained fluency in German, English, and Latin in high school. Thus, by the time he graduated from college, Hammarskjöld had acquired seven languages in addition to his native Swedish. This was important to him, too, partly because he enjoyed reading poetry, short stories, and novels from around the world.

In particular, he was drawn to the verse of Emily Dickinson and the short stories of Katherine Mansfield, literature he enthusiastically recommended to others. He also enjoyed reading Hermann Hesse, Joseph Conrad, and Cervantes. Hammarskjöld's other cultural pursuits included concerts—he had a soft spot for the compositions of Vivaldi and Hindemith—and art exhibits, particularly those showcasing the French impressionists.

In respect to his private life, Hammarskjöld still lived at the castle with his parents rather than staying on campus with other students or securing a flat of his own. As a result, he had little interaction with his peers, at least of an informal nature. In a few cases, however, he did form platonic acquaintances with other young men while continuing to avoid involvements with women.

"He preferred to spend an hour debating with his philosophy or literature professor over a cup of hot chocolate to arguing about the attractiveness of various girl students over a stein of foaming ale," writes Israel Levine.[16]

Not surprisingly, most of the other students, as one writer put it, "kept their distance from him," although Jon Söderblom, the Archbishop's son and Hammarskjöld's childhood neighbor, remained his ally throughout their college days.[17] Later in life, Söderblom spoke admiringly of Hammarskjöld's loyalty to their relationship, while conceding that his friend did indeed keep the other students at arms' length.

Sympathetic biographers have implied that Hammarskjöld's refusal to take part in ordinary social activities, as well as his apparent decision to eschew sexual intimacy with women, was because he chose to live at home with his parents and was therefore constrained by his surroundings. Others have suggested that Hammarskjöld may have desired the companionship of his peers, but that they refused to oblige; they may have cast him aside because his father had been unpopular during the war or because his family lived in an aristocratic setting, thereby sparking their envy. One writer even claimed that Hammarskjöld's classmates were "spiritually and religiously unawakened," and thus spoke "a language foreign to his soul."[18] It is not at all apparent that any of these reasons were responsible for his impaired relationships. The truth is, Hammarskjöld had never related well to others, not since he first stepped outside the castle to begin kindergarten. In all likelihood, his college classmates avoided him simply because they believed he did not want their company.

One known fact about the late teen period of Hammarskjöld's life is that his decision to largely forgo contact with those of his own age forced him to become more self-reliant than ever before, a development that was not entirely without benefit. More precisely, his ability to exist with little social contact while studying for long stretches of time allowed him to avoid stressful social obligations and amass an impressive catalog of scholarly credentials. Even so, he was painfully lonely during this time, so lonesome that he contemplated suicide, according to W. H. Auden, who based his conclusion on Hammarskjöld's diaries from this period.[19] It would seem that Hammarskjöld's self-imposed isolation was not altogether willful and certainly did not satisfy him emotionally, spiritually, or sexually. Consequently, previous biographers' efforts to portray him as a highly evolved being who existed in a perpetual state of inner peace and whose wisdom was beyond that of his peers is contradicted by his own recollections of emptiness, confusion, despair, and loneliness.

Brightening Hammarskjöld's drab personal life, on the other hand, was his relationship with his mother, with whom he shared much of his time when he was not at school. By this point, Hjalmar was spending his days at the office and his nights in the castle's library, thereby leaving little time for his son and wife, perhaps by design. By all accounts, Hjalmar became increasingly bitter and reclusive as he aged. The other Hammarskjöld sons were no longer in the home, having gone on to pursue their own careers. Although there were occasional houseguests, such as Sundar Singh, the Indian mystic, and Rabindranath Tagore, the Indian writer and Nobel Prize recipient, the youngest Hammarskjöld spent most of his hours with Agnes, as he had done since childhood.

The handful of male friendships he developed during his undergraduate years usually consisted of skiing or hiking partners. More often, Hammarskjöld trekked alone through the mountains, carrying a thermos of coffee and a book. During stops, he would read, then try to mentally organize and memorize the book's content, a task at which he was adept because he had a photographic memory. This is not to say that he was so intellectual as to be oblivious to the grandeur surrounding him. He was captivated by the beauty of the Swedish mountains and he took great pleasure in communing with nature, which for him was a means of attaining a sense of refuge. As well, it provided him with the opportunity to reflect upon and transcend his dysphoric life as a student.

"At some time all of us need tranquility and perspective," Hammarskjöld once told an acquaintance. "In the Swedish mountains one achieves solitude and distance, not by fleeing from reality, but by meeting a reality other than that of the workaday world."[20]

His undergraduate career was impressive but brief, concluding after only two years of study. Hammarskjöld was awarded a baccalaureate degree with honors at the age of nineteen.

The next step in his academic ascent took place at Stockholm University and involved the subject of political economy. Although he had planned to attend law school after receiving his undergraduate degree, his father persuaded him to first obtain a master's degree in economics. Law school could wait, Hjalmar told him. So Dag Hammarskjöld, ever the obeisant son, entered graduate school in Stockholm, where he dove into economics with his characteristic zeal. To his liking, he met other serious-minded, no-nonsense students like himself, kindred spirits who hoped to change the world. One of these was Sven Stolpe, who was to become a renowned religious writer and literary critic, as well as Chancellor of the Swedish Catholic Academy.

Stolpe first met Hammarskjöld at the Sigtuna Foundation, a cultural and religious retreat located in a picturesque village near Stockholm. When Stolpe caught sight of him, Hammarskjöld was strolling along a lakefront arcade, his face buried in a book. Shortly thereafter, the two men struck up a conversation, and Stolpe soon found himself admiring Hammarskjöld's brilliance and civility. In the end, they became friends for life, with Stolpe eventually writing a respectful account of the religious facets of Hammarskjöld's life. Although Hammarskjöld was no doubt drawn to the spiritual realm, political matters fascinated him even more, especially while he was a graduate student.

During his three years at Stockholm University, he not only studied economics but also kept an eye on international affairs, most notably on the pacifist movements that were springing up in many nations as a consequence of World War I. He also kept a watch on the League of Nations, which at this point appeared to be making progress, thus causing him to conclude prematurely that his father's doubts about the organization had been misplaced. He also stayed abreast of new and provocative ideas in the intelligentsia, ideas stimulated by the times.

Providentially, Hammarskjöld attended graduate school during a period of infectious optimism and social progress, an epoch known as the Golden Twenties in Germany, the Jazz Age in France, and the Roaring Twenties in the United States. It was the era of Greta Garbo and Marlene Dietrich, of Marc Chagall and Piet Mondrian, of George Gershwin and Béla Bartok. Placing the war far behind them, people were daring to celebrate life once again, convinced the world would never again devolve into a warring mass of chaos and tragedy. In this spirited age, hope ruled the day.

In this vibrant milieu Hammarskjöld and his colleagues debated the theories of Sigmund Freud and the theses of Karl Marx. They also discussed Sweden's recurrent problem of poverty, one that had existed since the 1850s. On this subject, some students argued that communism, as practiced in Russia, was the only reasonable solution, while others insisted that destitution could best be eliminated through a nontotalitarian approach. Hammarskjöld remained unconvinced that communism or socialism was the answer, although he was curious about the ideas being put forth by the up-and-coming economist John Maynard Keynes.

A British scholar and long-time member of the Bloomsbury group, Keynes was an independent, assertive man in his personal and professional life. He had enjoyed, as a young man, a sexual relationship with another man that lasted seven years. Although Keynes later married a Russian ballerina, he never attempted to conceal or deny his earlier gay romance. His theories of political economics, as well as his principled condemnation of the Big Four, rendered him controversial for years to come.

During World War I, Keynes, a high-level official in the British Treasury, managed the financial end of the war for the Crown. Then, after the armistice, he participated in the peace talks in Paris, ultimately walking out on them because he believed the Big Four were insisting that Germany make war reparations far beyond what the country could possibly afford. In a book he wrote at the time, *The Economic Consequences of the Peace,* Keynes, according to historian

Thomas Cowan, "argued for the economic unity of Europe, exposed the selfishness on the part of the Allies in framing the reparations, and demonstrated how the enormous sum involved was not only unrealistic but devastating to world economic stability."[21] Predictably, the book became an overnight sensation.

During the following several years, Keynes published more texts, bold works that challenged the traditional laissez-faire approach to economic growth. That is to say, they took issue with the premise that government should stay out of domestic economic matters, even during periods of recession. Keynes proposed the opposite, namely that government should directly intervene, particularly during slumps, to stimulate the economy. When the economy stabilized, he posited, the government could relieve itself of any debt it might have incurred along the way. This idea, today referred to as "deficit spending," revolutionized the field of economics in the twentieth century.

Although not a strict Keynesian, Hammarskjöld adhered to many of the economist's propositions. Although he was not a leftist in the strict sense of the word, Hammarskjöld was attracted to certain elements of socialism. The system appealed to his sense of social justice, especially to his belief that a nation should ensure that the needs of the entire citizenry are fulfilled, not just those of the elite, a view he retained throughout his lifetime. He also came to embrace pacifism and gained a renewed respect for the theory and practice of political neutrality. Hammarskjöld was a bona fide Swede in outlook. Even so, he never became a full-fledged socialist, despite the fact that Sweden was leaning heavily in this direction.

In 1928, three years after entering Stockholm University, Hammarskjöld received his masters degree in economics. He was twenty-two years old at the time and considered "razor-sharp."[22] His next step was to enter law school at Uppsala University, his father's alma mater.

While studying jurisprudence at Uppsala, Hammarskjöld continued to live with his parents at the castle. As had been the case in years past, he did not date, although he often had the chance. To encourage him, his mother's friends, without his knowledge or consent, would arrange for unmarried women to be available to him at dinner parties and other gatherings. Of course, Hammarskjöld, a well-bred young man, was invariably cordial to them, but never did he attempt to maneuver these contrived social encounters into romantic interludes.

Hammarskjöld continued to impress his professors and colleagues alike with his scholarly achievements, in time emerging as the unrivaled golden boy of Stockholm University's law school. Even Hjalmar had taken to praising his son by this time, the former Prime Minister telling a friend, "If I had Dag's brains, I could've gone far."[23] But although the youngest Hammarskjöld had clearly attained academic excellence, he still suffered self-doubt. He also struggled to live an authentic existence, writing in his journal at the time, "What you have to attempt—to be yourself."[24]

His inner struggles notwithstanding, Hammarskjöld received his degree in jurisprudence in 1930, following which he ventured rather hesitantly into the world. It was a world that had changed dramatically since he entered law school.

The Great Depression had descended like a storm cloud over the Western world, and Sweden, suffering immensely like other nations, desperately needed fresh, innovative leadership well-versed in economics and the law. For this reason, the King of Sweden, as well as the Swedish government, welcomed Hammarskjöld's debut in the professional world. They believed the twenty-five-year-old *wunderkind* could help rescue the nation from the clutches of poverty. They appointed him Secretary of the Royal Commission on Unemployment, a prestigious assignment that surprised no one but annoyed a handful of critics due to Hammarskjöld's youth and lack of policy-making experience. Nevertheless, the public had always assumed that he would someday become the torchbearer of his family's legacy of distinguished service to king and country, so most naysayers felt it wise to keep their counsel. Hammarskjöld accepted the assignment at once and set to work helping the nation solve its financial woes.

THE GREAT DEPRESSION

In 1930, the year that Hammarskjöld began working for the government, his father retired as Governor of Uppland, the nation's largest province. Subsequently, Hjalmar, Agnes, and Dag moved to Stockholm, where they lived in an elegant apartment owned by the Nobel Foundation, one overlooking the stately park that encircled the Royal Library. By this time, the other three Hammarskjöld sons had established their own residences and high-profile careers: Bo was serving in the Ministry of Social Welfare, Åke was acting as Registrar at the International Court of Justice at The Hague, and Sten was working for *The New York Times* in Manhattan.

In Dag's new administrative position, he struggled to answer crucial questions about Sweden's rising jobless rate, routinely spending his waking hours poring over volumes of statistics housed in countless government offices and libraries. Never before had these figures been examined so meticulously and comprehensively. Completing his research several months later, he wrote a detailed report illuminating the Great Depression's impact on the Swedish economy, most notably its effect on unemployment patterns, and proposed realistic methods for reversing the nation's headlong course toward financial ruin. His suggestions were heeded. Shortly after he released his report, the government decided to act on his recommendations, with the document itself impressing economists throughout Sweden. It even won the respect of a circle of brilliant young economists whose innovative approach was known as the Stockholm School.

Deriving its inspiration largely from the ideas of John Maynard Keynes, most notably from his books *A Treatise on Money* and *The End of the Laissez-Faire,* the Stockholm School was also influenced by the propositions of Swedish socialist and philosophy professor Ernst Wigforss. A leading figure in the nation's Social Democratic Party, Wigforss would go on to play an instrumental role in Hammarskjöld's career. Before long, the Stockholm School embraced Hammarskjöld himself, who quickly became its principal source of intellectual energy.

Tensions were mounting throughout the world at this time. In Germany, Adolf Hitler was garnering popular support, being named chancellor in 1932 and shortly thereafter arming his nation for war, a turn of events that troubled the Swedish people. Adding to their worries, a Swedish tycoon, Ivan Kreuger, whose companies produced nearly half of the world's matches, committed suicide in Paris that same year because he was about to be exposed for falsifying his companies' records. As sometimes happens in financial scandals, his suicide triggered the collapse of several related industries in Sweden. The upshot of these destabilizing events, coming as they did on the heels of the Great Depression, is that the Social Democrats assumed control of the government. Literally overnight, the political scene began to change.

Among the Party's first acts was the installation of Ernst Wigforss as Minister of Finance. In this capacity, the distinguished socialist enjoyed a bird's-eye view of Sweden's economic life, including Hammarskjöld's work on the Royal Commission on Unemployment. Wigforss was already familiar with Hammarskjöld's high ethical standards and strict self-discipline, as well as with his intellectual gifts. The new Minister of Finance hoped to someday make use of the talented young economist.

Hammarskjöld likewise respected Wigforss, although his contact with the dignitary was limited. This was because Hammarskjöld spent his days coaching government officials on how best to implement the findings of his study on unemployment. To further his career, he submitted one of the study's appendices, along with an elaboration on it, to Stockholm University and asked that it be considered his doctoral dissertation in economics, and the school agreed. It was in this way that he was called upon to defend his dissertation in 1933, a performance that was anything but stellar.

During the examination Hammarskjöld became extremely anxious and inhibited whenever a problem required an innovative, unorthodox solution. Under such circumstances, he was unable to think creatively and his thought processes became muddled and confused. Hammarskjöld was not impressed with the examination process itself. "It was just a circus," he later said. "(T)he ritual seemed to me morally inferior."[25] Years later, however, when he pulled his dissertation off the shelf to peruse it once again, he confessed to a friend that he had difficulty understanding his own words. Even one of his more sympathetic biographers described the dissertation as "thoroughly dreary."[26]

Regardless, Hammarskjöld received his doctorate, although he did not receive the university's highest honor, *laudatur,* as he had hoped. Although he had derived satisfaction from his schooling, he decided that his career from this point forward would involve hands-on, applied work, not theoretical activities. In the opinion of Gunnar Myrdal, one of the scholars who administered Hammarskjöld's oral exam in economics, this was because Hammarskjöld knew that he was too mentally constrained to be an effective researcher.

Such inner inhibitions notwithstanding, Hammarskjöld's career continued to flourish. Upon receiving his doctorate, he was offered an Assistant Professorship in Political Economy at Stockholm University, where he began teaching part-time. In addition, he continued serving as Secretary of the Royal Commission on Unemployment. He then relinquished both jobs so he could assume new and more pressing responsibilities.

In 1935, he accepted the position of Secretary of the National Bank of Sweden, the world's oldest note-issuing bank, in which capacity he displayed his unique brand of brilliance. So impressive was his performance that, a year later, Ernst Wigforss tapped him to serve as Permanent Undersecretary in the Ministry of Finance, where Hammarskjöld, as always, labored to help the nation regain its financial footing. Ultimately, the public judged him successful in his task.

Sweden, within a few short years, became the first country in the world to fully recover from the Great Depression, largely because Hammarskjöld and his associates devised a novel economic system, which fused collectivism with individualism. Using a Fabian approach, they worked constructively within Sweden's existing political and economic structures to bring about change rather than acting outside the system in a more radical Marxist fashion. The result is that the Swedes systematically transformed their nation into a near-welfare state, albeit one with a free-market economy. In the process, they temporarily placed their country in debt so as to ultimately save it. "They initiated the first program of consciously planned deficits in history," explains author Michael Harrington.[27] They achieved a zero unemployment rate, as well as one of the highest per capita incomes in the world. Hammarskjöld, who was credited with coining the term "planned economy" during this period, enjoyed widespread acclaim as the principal architect of this innovative, efficient scheme. He was praised on other counts as well, most notably on his work habits, which were rather excessive.

He routinely arrived at his office at nine in the morning and worked until six at night, at which time he joined his mother and father at the Nobel apartment for dinner. Later, at nine o'clock in the evening when his mother retired, Hammarskjöld would often return to his office and work until five the next morning. Thus, he literally toiled night and day, in this way accomplishing far more than his married colleagues but at a cost to himself in that he had little in the way of a personal life, not that this necessarily bothered him. Indeed, his decision to work at such a relentless pace may have served in part to relieve him of those social obligations he preferred to avoid. Even as he

forfeited the opportunity to meet new people and brush up on his social skills, he managed to hone his interpersonal abilities in other
ways.

During his tenure at the Ministry of Finance, for instance, Hammarskjöld worked hard to sharpen his diplomatic adeptness, developing in the process a remarkable capacity for bringing together opposing elements within large groups. His subordinates genuinely liked
him, as did his superior, Ernst Wigforss, with whom he got along fa-
mously. Years later, Hammarskjöld described Wigforss with true affection as his "second father."[28] Hammarskjöld's upbringing as the
Prime Minister's son had definitely prepared him for a cooperative
relationship with a government leader of Wigforss's prominence.

Although Hammarskjöld possessed numerous talents, including
diplomatic skills, he also displayed limitations of a sort. He was not a
quick study, although he was able to assimilate vast amounts of material if given sufficient time. He also had difficulty expressing himself
clearly in writing, as his dissertation had revealed. Furthermore, while
his colleagues thought they knew him well, a misperception Hammarskjöld is said to have encouraged and even exploited at times, in
reality they knew nothing about his inner life and very little about his
private life. In large part, this was because it was still restricted to his
family's apartment in Stockholm, and especially to his mother.

As had been the case since childhood, Hammarskjöld remained
tied to Agnes during this period, his late-twenties to mid-thirties, the
bond between them strong and unwavering. Each day, he presented
her with a bouquet of fresh-cut flowers and was always certain to be
home in time for dinner with her. On those days when meetings at the
Ministry of Finance ran overtime, he would take a taxi home rather
than make her wait, despite the fact that their apartment was only a
fifteen-minute walk from his office. Agnes, by all accounts, continued to be the central figure in his life.

Alluding to this sustained attachment, one of Hammarskjöld's acquaintances, Sten Söderberg, once described Hammarskjöld as Agnes's
"gentleman-in-waiting,"[29] while a less charitable observer referred to
him as her "stay-at-home daughter."[30] The young Swede certainly
was not an out-and-about young man.

Hammarskjöld did not have a sex life as far as anyone could tell.
He still refused to become romantically involved with women, going
so far as to attend important social events alone, without the custom-

ary female companion on his arm. This did not stop friends of the family from trying, as before, to arrange romantic encounters for him. In one instance, they brought him together with an adorable young woman they were sure would be the right match for him. Lovely, well-educated—she had a PhD—and the daughter of a successful financier, she was in their view perfection in human form. But Hammarskjöld showed no interest in her, a reaction prompting his baffled friends to ask why he had not been taken with the woman.

"She didn't appreciate T. S. Eliot," he replied.[31]

In another episode a few years later when Hammarskjöld had secured his own flat in Stockholm, a young woman wishing to obtain a job as a secretary misrepresented herself as a maid and gained entrance to his apartment. There, she climbed into bed and waited for him to return from work. When Hammarskjöld arrived, he was appalled by the surprise awaiting him, pulling the woman from his bed and restraining her while a friend called the police. In an odd twist, he refused to stay in the flat, and moved out the next day.

Understandably, such quirky occurrences did little to prevent his sexual disposition from becoming the topic of gossip. By any standard, it was unconventional, if not downright odd, for a public figure of his standing to be unmarried, childless, and apparently celibate. Nevertheless, the prevailing assumption at the time, and a mistaken one, was that a homosexual man was invariably effeminate, and that he either wished to be a woman or was afraid of women. In these respects, Hammarskjöld did not fit the stereotype. Although he was poised and refined, most people did not think of him as effeminate, nor did he give the impression of being fearful of the opposite sex. Seizing this fact, a handful of his acquaintances tried strenuously over the years to use his purported masculinity to somehow prove his heterosexuality, although, often as not, they undermined their own efforts by also mentioning his total lack of erotic desire for women. In the passage that follows, Sven Stolpe, after Hammarskjöld's death, sought to defend his old friend against the persistent rumor of homosexuality, but in the course of his argument made a comment that, rather than putting the innuendo to rest, unwittingly lent support to the view that Hammarskjöld might well have been gay. Writes Stolpe,

> He was masculine all through, there was nothing effeminate in his nature. He was not afraid of women, and could speak expertly on feminine beauty, yet I sometimes felt that for all his

polite talk at parties he never visually discriminated between a
shapely woman and, say, a sofa or a chair.[32]

Based on what is known about this and later periods of Hammarskjöld's life, it seems obvious that he was anything but heterosexual. He appeared to go out of his way to make it clear that he did not find the opposite sex even remotely desirable. The question, then, is whether he was homosexual or asexual, a matter which will be explored in greater depth at a later point.

Despite his heavy workload, a workload previous biographers have pointed to rather disingenuously as yet another reason he did not date women, he found ample time to escape into the Swedish mountains, especially when he was stressed. During getaways of this sort, he would be gone for days at a time without telling others in advance, including his colleagues at the Ministry of Finance. Most often, he took another man with him.

On one memorable excursion, Hammarskjöld and a companion, Erik Swartling, bicycled northward toward the nation's border with Norway. Along the way, the two men stopped in the village of Elvirum and took a room at a local inn. In this settlement so far north as to be barren of most vegetation, Hammarskjöld and Swartling scrutinized the town's layout and decided it would make a safe stopover if Hitler's expansionist aims were to someday make necessary their escape from Sweden. Such was the air of catastrophe hovering over Europe at the time.

On other trips, Hammarskjöld and a companion traveled beyond the Arctic Circle. Sometimes they even went farther north, to Lapland.

When he was not unwinding with a friend in the great outdoors, he could nearly always be found at the family's Stockholm apartment, where he read several works of fiction each week and tended to his parents' needs. Now and then, he also took his mother to a concert or an art exhibit.

Hammarskjöld apparently did not keep a journal during these years, the only time in his adult life he did not feel the need to record his feelings and reflections. Consequently, little is known about his musings at this point. He also did not seem overly concerned with spiritual matters, again for the first time in his life, although he remained in contact with his friend Sven Stolpe, with whom he corresponded on a regular basis. Hammarskjöld sent him poignant letters in which he shared his thoughts on Stolpe's religious writings, which had begun being published to great acclaim. As did the public, Hammarskjöld enjoyed them immensely, just as he enjoyed life itself. His family and friends later stated that these seemed to be his happiest years, a time when he appeared to be genuinely, deeply satisfied. One thing that did not bring him joy, however, was media attention.

Hammarskjöld barely had a public persona despite being an important figure in government, not to mention being a Hammarskjöld. This was because he was intimidated by the scrutiny of the press and kept reporters at a distance. When he sought advice from his father on the matter, Hjalmar told him that, as a high-profile official in the Ministry of Finance, he would simply have to get used to life in a fish bowl. Hammarskjöld would have none of it. He steadfastly refused to grant interviews in which his personal life might be discussed, a guardedness that did little to allay suspicions that he might be homosexual.

Despite Hammarskjöld's avoidance of the media, by this point in the late 1930s he was considered Sweden's top economist. The public also regarded him as a patriot who was serving his nation diligently by helping draft legislation designed to keep its unemployment rate among the lowest in the world. Furthermore, his activities now brought him into frequent contact with the foreign office, since his economic initiatives were increasingly tied to Sweden's foreign policy, with the office staff likewise applauding his astuteness and devotion to country. Despite Hammarskjöld's loyalty, however, he had misgivings about one of the nation's leading sources of income, namely, its munitions industry.

By this time Sweden had become a leading manufacturer of steel products, including weaponry. Disturbingly, the Scandinavian nation was now reaping enormous profits by selling munitions to nations under attack by Hitler as he prepared to steamroll his way across Europe and as surrounding nations scrambled to protect themselves. At the same time, Sweden refused to commit to either side in what was shaping up to be a major showdown. Understandably, Hammarskjöld found his country's practice of enriching itself through such means troubling. After all, the nation prided itself on being a country devoted to pacifism.

He was disillusioned, too, by the League of Nations' action, or more precisely, by its inaction, in preventing those events that were clearly leading toward armed confrontation. At the same moment Hitler was preparing to swallow up Europe, a fellow dictator, Benito Mussolini, was ordering Italian troops to invade Abyssinia, an African kingdom known today as Ethiopia. In response to Il Duce's belligerence, the League of Nations called for sanctions against Italy, but Mussolini merely scoffed at the coalition's demands. Obviously, stronger measures would be needed to bring about the dictator's compliance, but the League's member nations decided to go no farther. Instead, they remained on the sidelines as Abyssinia fell, a discouraging moment marking the beginning of the end for the League of Nations.

During this bleak period Hammarskjöld and his parents gathered around the radio each evening and listened to reports of the League's failure to act in a decisive fashion. When it became evident that the coalition was unwilling to stop the lethal slide toward war, Dag became demoralized and his father is said to have wept. The demise of the League of Nations was not the only reason for despair. In 1937 Åke Hammarskjöld died of rheumatic fever at age forty-two, his premature death stunning his colleagues at the International Court of Justice and devastating the Hammarskjöld family. Several months later, Dag became further dispirited, this time for political reasons, as he watched German troops invade Austria, then march into Czechoslovakia and Poland, a series of acts that prompted surrounding nations to take up arms in the accelerating fight. Finally, in 1939, he witnessed the outbreak of World War II and knew that suffering would soon come to millions across Europe and beyond.

THE WAR YEARS

In 1940, Hitler's troops invaded Belgium, Holland, and two Scandinavian nations, Norway and Denmark, a startling turn of events that placed Sweden in a position of utmost vulnerability. The Swedes, however, decided to hold firm to their policy of noninvolvement in foreign disputes despite the unsettling presence of Nazis on their doorstep.

Sadly, Agnes Hammarskjöld died that same year, a crushing blow to Dag. A truly agonizing moment in his life, he told friends that the world seemed to be collapsing around him. Perhaps it was for this reason that he rediscovered his spiritual side at this time, as well as renewing his practice of keeping a journal in which he wrote poetry and recorded his thoughts, feelings, and concerns.

Hammarskjöld was still at the Ministry of Finance during this dark period, while his brother Bo was serving as Undersecretary in the Ministry of Social Welfare. Together, the two worked hard to introduce meaningful reform designed to hasten Sweden's further transformation into a welfare state. Even so, neither brother joined the Social Democratic Party, nor, for that matter, considered himself a socialist. Instead, each remained a civil servant without party affiliation on the grounds that this would help prevent him from acquiring partisan prejudices. They were successful in maintaining their impartiality, and Dag, in particular, demonstrated remarkable objectivity the following year when his career took an unexpected turn.

While at the Ministry of Finance, he was concurrently appointed Chairman of the Board of the National Bank of Sweden, a state of affairs that delighted him but raised eyebrows in conservative quarters. Some feared that Hammarskjöld in this capacity would become the puppet of Ernst Wigforss, in effect handing the ardent socialist unprecedented control over the nation's economy. Others worried that holding both jobs—the first time in history one person had ever been asked to do so—would produce a conflict of interests. Still others fretted that the job demands would be far too great for one person to bear. Undeterred, Hammarskjöld accepted the challenge and quickly proved the hand-wringers wrong. Not only did he find the energy and ingenuity to perform both roles, but he performed them ethically and efficiently. Furthermore, he applied his favorite approach, Keynesian, which proved successful in stabilizing Sweden's economy during World War II.

More precisely, Hammarskjöld drafted a long-term economic plan for Sweden that combined deficit spending with price controls. He also arranged for financial aid to be funneled to those neighboring Scandinavian nations that were suffering the effects of war, most notably by devising a system whereby his government could provide nonmilitary support to Finland while remaining true to its policy of political neutrality. As well, he knowingly put his life on the line to help beleaguered Norway, among other deeds participating in a hazardous operation designed to preserve its rightful government.

"It will mean personal danger," Wigforss told Hammarskjöld about the mission, "and it must remain top secret."[33] The mission to which the Minister of Finance was referring consisted of several meetings with Norway's government-in-exile, the aim being to get Swedish money into its hands. Norwegian officials had decided to set up operations in England because their homeland had fallen under Nazi control. Hammarskjöld offered these uprooted leaders economic advice and financial support at meetings set up in secret locations across Sweden, with the final conference of this type scheduled to take place in England.

For this meeting, Hammarskjöld and a handful of expatriated Norwegian officials boarded a large transport plane late one night at an airport near Stockholm. Once onboard, they were issued parachutes and life vests since it was conceivable their aircraft would become a target while en route to England, a harrowing possibility that soon became a reality. Indeed, as the Swedish plane emerged from heavy cloud cover over the North Sea, the German *Luftwaffe* detected it and moved in for the kill. Taking swift evasive action, the Swedish plane pitched violently as it sought to enshroud itself in another bank of clouds until finally it succeeded in escaping the Germans. Throughout the hair-raising ordeal, the stunned passengers stared helplessly through the plane's windows into the blackness enveloping them—everyone, that is, except Hammarskjöld, who kept his nose buried in a sixteenth-century classic he had brought with him. "There's nothing like French poetry and a strong cigar to calm the nerves," he told a shaken passenger, a Norwegian diplomat, once the plane was back on course.[34]

The actions of the Swedish government, by comparison, were not always so courageous. While claiming neutrality, Sweden furnished naval escorts for German ships in the Baltic Sea, as well as allowing German troops and supplies to cross Sweden by train on their way to Norway. Despite the government's insistence that it had little choice lest Sweden itself be invaded, these actions caused critics to accuse it of collaboration with the Nazis.

Even as Sweden sought to pacify Germany, it helped desperate Jews seeking to escape Hitler's gas chambers. From Denmark alone, 5,000 Jews whose arrest the Nazis had ordered found refuge in Sweden in a clandestine operation orchestrated by the Danish underground and the Swedish government. A non-Jewish Swedish aristocrat, Raoul Wallenberg, was dispatched by the government to Budapest in 1944 in a last-ditch attempt to rescue what remained of Hungary's

Jewish population. Ultimately, Wallenberg saved the lives of 100,000 Jewish men, women, and children before he was arrested and never heard from again.

At precisely the same time the Swedish aristocrat Wallenberg was rescuing Hungarian Jews, a crucial conference was taking place in Washington, DC, at a mansion known as Dumbarton Oaks. There, officials from the Soviet Union, China, England, and the United States brainstormed various ways to prevent future wars. While the four powers did not dispute the fact that the League of Nations had been a washout, their consensus was that a new organization could meet with success if it were to scrupulously avoid the League's failures. From these talks the United Nations was born, its charter drafted by the delegates from scores of countries in April 1945, and finalized two months later in a ceremony at the historic San Francisco Opera House. The following October, after the war was over, the UN charter was ratified, with Hammarskjöld and his friends in Stockholm celebrating the event. Hammarskjöld, who believed an earnest attempt should again be made to secure and preserve world peace, saw the advent of the United Nations as an important step in the right direction.

He was also pleased to find his own activities in the postwar era bringing him into even greater contact with Sweden's Foreign Office. This came about because his efforts to help the nation reestablish itself financially were by necessity tied to its trade relations with other countries, thus thrusting him into the realm of international affairs.

Among other roles, he became an advisor to the Swedish Cabinet in 1945, overseeing all matters pertaining to the nation's financial security. Not long afterward, he was named Undersecretary of Financial Affairs and transferred to the Foreign Office, then, the following year, entrusted with principal responsibility for negotiating a crucial trade agreement with the United States. Next, in 1947, the government dispatched him to Paris to help forge the Marshall Plan.

Now that his actions were directly affecting the economies of other nations, Hammarskjöld found himself spending substantial time in the French capitol, the hub of foreign relations in that era. All the same, he made it a point to return to Stockholm each weekend so he could look in on his father, who was in his eighties and, although frail, still reviewing books for the Nobel Prize. Dag usually stayed at home with him during these visits, although occasionally he attended a concert, particularly if it featured the works of Mahler or Stravinsky. He also made frequent entries in his journal, and, as had been the case throughout his life, read voraciously. Most of all, though, he discussed with his father the evolution of the United Nations, the one topic that captured both men's attention.

THE UNITED NATIONS

In its initial years, the United Nations was impressive. Unlike the defunct League of Nations, it enjoyed the participation of nearly all of the world's major powers. At start-up, fifty countries signed its charter, including those as variant as the Soviet Union and the United States. Also unlike the League, the UN assigned itself a truly sweeping task. Its members decided that its role should not be limited to mediating conflicts that were already underway but should include a mechanism through which it could prevent such disputes in the first place. This it hoped to accomplish by creating programs that would enhance social and economic cooperation at the global level. Such were its laudable goals.

The main body of the UN was the General Assembly, which consisted of the delegates from all of the member nations. The Assembly's purpose was to deliberate issues of international importance brought before it by representatives from around the world. The Assembly, in turn, was divided into five agencies, the most critical being the Security Council, whose job it was to preserve world peace by resolving political quarrels that were likely to escalate to armed conflict or had already done so. Other agencies included the International Court of Justice, put in place to settle legal disputes between countries, the Economic and Social Council, designed to safeguard human rights and encourage the prosperity of member nations, and the Trusteeship Council, formed to protect the interests of small, vulnerable territories. The remaining agency, the Secretariat, was created to assist the aforementioned divisions in carrying out their duties.

The most influential staff position was Secretary-General, the UN's chief administrator. This official exercised more power than anyone else in the organization. Among other responsibilities, the Secretary-General decided which issues were of sufficient importance to take before the General Assembly for deliberation, as well as exercising the authority to intervene personally in international disputes. In the

UN's formative years, however, the role of Secretary-General was rather ill-defined, and often controversial, as Trygve Lie, the first person to hold the post, discovered.

An attorney by training, Lie was Norway's Foreign Minister before he found himself nominated to the lofty UN post. His subsequent election, however, was both the beginning and the end of his triumph. As soon as he started the job, Lie began making formidable enemies due to his tendency to be highly opinionated and outspoken.

Never one to sit back and simply monitor the operation of the United Nations, the new Secretary-General involved himself in many of the major political disputes of the day, about which he would make public statements on behalf of the world community. As often as not, this dismayed his UN colleagues who did not always agree with his views and certainly did not appreciate his decision to serve as their spokesperson. They considered his role to be that of coordinator, not mouthpiece for the organization.

The dawn of the Cold War era worsened matters, and the Soviet Union and the United States were invariably at each other's throats. Routinely, the Soviets would denounce Lie whenever he supported the United States' position on an issue, dismissing him as a stooge, a flunky of corporate America. When he sided with the Soviets, on the other hand, the United States would brand him a Communist sympathizer and a traitor to the cause of democracy. Even France and Great Britain condemned him whenever he adopted a stance that was at odds with their politico-economic interests in Asia or Africa. In such ways, Lie came to be disparaged on all sides.

The situation managed to deteriorate still further. As Lie was wrapping up his five-year term in 1950, the Security Council decided to renominate him for a three-year extension but the Soviet delegate refused to endorse him. Brushing aside the Soviet rejection, the Council proceeded with its plan to submit the Norwegian's name to a vote of the General Assembly, and did, in fact, succeed in having Lie reelected for three more years. The upshot was that the USSR refused to recognize him as the rightful Secretary-General and thereafter would not work with him. Lie, however, remained at his post, albeit illegitimately, because the Korean War was in progress and he believed it unwise to step down at such a precarious time. By November 1952, however, he had become such a political lame duck that he tendered his resignation, arranging for his departure to take place five months later. It was during the following spring, when the search for his predecessor began and when the future of the UN looked especially dim, that Hammarskjöld's name came to the fore.

Dag had been serving dutifully as Undersecretary of Sweden's Foreign Office, then as Secretary-General of the same agency, and finally as a Minister to the Cabinet during those stormy years when the UN was plagued by internecine warfare. After that, in 1951, he found himself involved with the United Nations when the Swedish government appointed him vice-chairman of its delegation to the Sixth Regular Session of the UN General Assembly in Paris. As could be expected given his enormous respect for the organization, Hammarskjöld reveled in the experience. The following year, he was even more delighted when he was appointed acting chairman of the Swedish delegation to the UN's Seventh Regular Session in New York City. Although he was enthralled by his brief contact with the global federation, however, those at the UN were not entranced by him. Few staffers took notice of the pale, soft-spoken Swede. This is why it came as such a shock to him when he received a phone call late one evening at his Stockholm apartment from an Associated Press reporter asking if he planned to accept the nomination of Secretary-General of the United Nations. Amused, Hammarskjöld thought it was an April Fool's joke and wondered aloud who might be behind the prank.

Of course, when he realized the news was real, he took the matter very seriously. Hammarskjöld did not want to be Secretary-General, convinced the position was far beyond his experience and capability. He also could not understand how he had come to be the candidate, since the Security Council, to his knowledge, barely knew he existed. That, however, was precisely why he had been nominated.

The truth is that UN power brokers believed they had made a grievous mistake in choosing Trygve Lie to be Secretary-General. The bellicose Norwegian had proven far too divisive. Accordingly, they decided to nominate a mild-mannered bureaucrat, a conforming, benign administrator who would remain behind the scenes and oversee the day-to-day operation of the organization in an inoffensive manner. The French delegate proposed Hammarskjöld's name and the Soviet delegate seconded it. The Security Council believed it had selected a nonthreatening civil servant who would not make waves.

Meanwhile, during the first week of April 1953, as Hammarskjöld's nomination was being readied for a vote in Manhattan, the forty-eight-year-old Swede visited his aged father in the hospital and asked for his blessing. Next day, Dag paid a brief visit to his mother's grave, then met at length with the King of Sweden, whose advice he sought. Finally, when the announcement was made that Hammarskjöld had been officially elected to the post of Secretary-General by a unanimous vote of the General Assembly, he boarded a plane for New York to begin his new, and final, job.

Hammarskjöld quickly settled into urban life in Manhattan, leasing an apartment on Park Avenue and decorating it so sparsely that it looked unfurnished. It did boast a large collection of books, however, as well as a small number of African art objects and his mother's bureau, which was jarringly out of place in the contemporary, austere surroundings. The apartment also contained a handful of abstract paintings. Hammarskjöld's love of modern art eventually extended to his office walls and to the lobby of the United Nations building itself.

Hammarskjöld was pleased to discover that his staff was congenial and enthusiastic, but he was distraught by the visibility that came with the position. More to the point, he was taken aback by the media's renewed interest in his personal life. Since he had not been in office long enough to regale reporters with tales of his deeds as Secretary-General, the press focused on more intimate subjects and this distressed him. As had been the case in Sweden, he refused to reveal any information about himself other than that which was strictly professional, in effect seeking refuge behind his UN title. "In my new official capacity, the private man should disappear and the international public servant take his place," he said at the time.[35]

Hammarskjöld's efforts to deflect attention from his personal life did not stop the media from noting that he had never married, and this resurrected the gay question. When Matt Gordon, a United Nations press officer, began reciting to the press corps the high points of Hammarskjöld's career prior to being elected to the UN post, he was interrupted by a reporter who cried out that the new Secretary-General was also "a fairy!"[36] The press was not alone in speculating about Hammarskjöld's sexual orientation; UN staffers wondered as well, particularly during his first months in office. Such conjecture was fueled by Hammarskjöld's predecessor Trygve Lie, who was not among his admirers and who was convinced the new Secretary-General was a closeted homosexual.

As to whether Lie's speculation was correct and Hammarskjöld was indeed drawn to his own gender, the true nature of the new Secretary-General's sexual interests was not known with certainty at the time. This was often the case for public figures who did not discuss their sexual interests with others, concealed their sexual activities, or chose not to act on their desires at all. Nevertheless, given what is known today, a reasonable proposition is that Hammarskjöld was homosexual.

As previously noted in the discussion of his childhood, Hammarskjöld was an emotionally sensitive boy who eschewed the rough-and-tumble play of other boys in favor of less competitive, more aesthetic activities, such as writing poetry and reading. As the findings of UCLA researcher Richard Green's studies have shown, this pattern of interests and activities is commonly observed in boys who grow up to be gay.[37] An additional perspective, this one from traditional Freudian thought, points to the nature of the Hammarskjöld family's dynamics; specifically, to Dag's nurturing, larger-than-life mother and his cold, distant father, a combination that purportedly contributes to the development of a same-sex orientation. The more observable fact is that Hammarskjöld refused to date girls while he attended high school, and as an adult refused to date women while he attended college and law school. Still later, as a prominent figure in the arena of national and international politics, he refused to marry, unlike the vast majority of his peers and contrary to social custom and public expectation. Indeed, this was a man who was never known to have had sex with a woman, nor to have displayed a desire to do so. A case can therefore be made that Hammarskjöld was not sexually attracted to the opposite sex, but rather was drawn to his own gender; certainly he preferred to spend time in the company of other men. Although no single element noted here can be construed as a clear-cut indicator of his sexual orientation, these in combination with other aspects of his personality and lifestyle do lend support to the popular notion that he had an affinity for other men.

Regarding the public speculation that beset Hammarskjöld when he became the UN Secretary-General, he appeared shocked that anyone would even mention his sexuality. Although this may have been disingenuous on his part—he may have been feigning moral outrage so as to shame and silence his inquisitors—it is possible that the aristocratic Swede truly did not grasp that being a middle-aged man who evidently had never had sex with a woman rendered him something of a curiosity in Manhattan. It is also possible that he did not understand that it was de rigeur for a man of his public standing to have a wife and children, particularly in the United States in the conservative 1950s, and that by eschewing marriage and family he could be perceived as thumbing his nose at tradition. Then, too, he may not have realized that refusing to discuss basic features of his personal life made it look as if he had something to hide. And perhaps he was hiding something, even from himself.

Hammarskjöld may well have been one of those gay men who never allows himself to recognize that he is homosexual. To such a person, the thought is so unbearable that he spends his life running away from it. This occurs today in a certain portion of gay men and most likely occurred with greater frequency in Hammarskjöld's era, when same-sex relations were even more unacceptable.

Certainly it is true that Sweden, although currently one of the most sexually progressive nations in the world, was not nearly so tolerant when Hammarskjöld was a child. At the beginning of the twentieth century, Swedish authorities considered male homosexuality such a serious moral lapse that they outlawed it and this legislation remained on the books until the end of World War II. Even more disturbing, the Swedish march toward socialism that occurred during the first half of the twentieth century had, as one of its aims, the containment of same-sex love. Swedish authorities subscribed to the notion of eugenics that was gaining a foothold in parts of Europe at the time. In 1921, they funded the world's first facility dedicated to "purifying" the citizenry. Located in Hammarskjöld's hometown of Uppsala, the center was christened the "Institute for Racial Biology." The nation also enacted laws calling for the castration or sterilization of so-called perverts, along with the mentally retarded. It was in this inhospitable environment that Hammarskjöld, during his high school and college years, came of age, a milieu that was far from conducive to "coming out" as gay, either to oneself or to others.

Furthermore, in the 1930s, while he was an official in the Swedish government, the socialist goal of discouraging homosexuality gained added momentum as a result of an influential paper by Gunnar Myrdal. Echoing previous efforts to weed out gay men, Myrdal's report, says

Finnish author Jan Löfström, "offered a compelling presentation of the idea that the progress and prosperity of society could be promoted by rational, scientifically informed social engineering."[38] Among other points, Myrdal argued that the state should ensure that "sexuality and sexual health (become) a vehicle for the achievement of society's common good."[39] This perspective, moreover, persisted well into the 1940s and 1950s, during which time the Swedish government systematically campaigned for "family values," while disapproving of same-sex relations, its aim being to increase the size and wealth of the heterosexual citizenry. This pressure to marry and reproduce paralleled the "baby boom" taking place in the United States at precisely the same time.

Also erupting in both countries in the early 1950s, a period when Hammarskjöld lived in both of them, was a widespread "moral panic" stemming from the myth of homosexual seduction, the fallacious idea that gay men were inclined to recruit young, unsuspecting males and lead them into lives of sexual vice. In addition, the American government began investigating and firing government employees suspected of being homosexual on the grounds that they were susceptible to Communist influence. Because of such pernicious fictions, gay men in the two nations suffered needlessly.

Thus, in view of the oppressive, antigay times and places in which Hammarskjöld lived, it is reasonable to propose that he may have been gay but unable to accept and act on his desires. Of course, had he owned up to his same-sex nature, he probably would have felt far less lonely and been at greater peace with his life. Had he done so publicly while Secretary-General of the United Nations, however, it undoubtedly would have brought his political career to an end, mortified his aging father and older brothers, tainted the aristocratic Hammarskjöld name, and shamed his homeland. Hammarskjöld had much to lose by facing his apparent homosexuality, and perhaps it was largely for this reason that he turned a blind eye to it.

As for the inventive ways in which he may have convinced himself that he was "not gay" and was being truthful about the matter, two common practices of conflicted gay men come to mind. First, Hammarskjöld refused to discuss his sexual interests with other people, thereby protecting himself from the impact of such conversations. That is to say, incisive discussions of his sexuality might well have forced him to confront that which he had suppressed for so many

years. By avoiding such talks he could continue to evade the homosexual issue while being honest with himself and others in presenting
himself as a man who was not knowingly gay.

Second, he may have chosen to define homosexuality in such a
way that it excluded him; certainly the 1950s stereotypes of the gay
man were not those with which he would readily identify. Gay men
were popularly depicted as mincing, shallow, and inept figures or as
sexual predators inhabiting a netherworld of degenerates having nothing but contempt for society. Quite rightly, Hammarskjöld would
never view himself in such ways, and he may have interpreted this
lack of correspondence with cultural stereotypes as proof that he was
not gay.

In a similar manner, he may have paired the term "homosexual"
with participation in the sex act itself, such that he could deny being
gay because he was not actually making love to other men. By this
definition, his apparent abstinence, to his way of thinking, would
spare him the dreaded label. He could truthfully say, in the parlance
of the times, that he was not an "active homosexual."

Of course, the fact that Hammarskjöld never had sex with anyone,
so far as is known, brings up the possibility of asexuality. Could it
have been that he was not physically attracted to either gender? This
is highly unlikely, since true asexuality is rare and is nearly always in-
duced by a severe trauma, an emotional injury so devastating that it
forever quashes the sex drive. Furthermore, even in those exceptional
cases in which asexuality is present, the person so affected may nevertheless relate emotionally to the opposite sex. Yet Hammarskjöld
displayed a marked disinterest in women, instead preferring to spend
his time in the company of other men. In some instances, these were
gay men, such as the poet W. H. Auden, who described a sense of
kinship with the sensitive, secretive Swede.

"I loved the man from the moment I saw him," Auden wrote after
Hammarskjöld's death. "[P]resumptuous as it sounds, I felt certain of
a mutual sympathy between us, of an unexpressed dialogue beneath
our casual conversation."[40]

Hammarskjöld also made disclosures in his journals, such as the
one in which he recalls an emotional experience with another man, an
unidentified figure whom he fails to meet head-on, authentically. Disappointed in himself, Hammarskjöld writes, "How undisguised your
thick-skinned self-satisfied loneliness appeared before his naked ag-

ony as he struggled to make a living contact. How difficult you found it to help, when confronted in another by your own problem—uncorrupted."[41]

At this point, it should be noted that Hammarskjöld had friends and associates who thought very highly of him and who tried to smother the gay rumors that swirled around him. Certainly this was to be expected. Closeted or conflicted gay men, particularly those who were publicly prominent in mid-century, were invariably surrounded by colleagues who defended the honor of these men, meaning that they refuted the gay innuendo. Quite often, these were people who wanted to believe the homosexual man was actually heterosexual, because they were associated with him. They did not want be on cordial terms with a gay man, and, furthermore, were concerned that their professional reputations might suffer because of their involvement with such a person. Accordingly, the most expedient response was to vehemently deny the rumors. Unfortunately, in Hammarskjöld's case this was sometimes done rather harshly, even after his death, in spite of the fact that such speculation was altogether warranted.

"Stupid or malicious people sometimes made the vulgar assumption that, being unmarried, he must be homosexual," wrote Brian Urquhart a decade after Hammarskjöld's death.[42] Urquhart, a former Undersecretary-General of the United Nations and a longtime Hammarskjöld associate, wrote these words at a time when homosexuality was still viewed as an abysmal moral lapse, hence his reference to people making the "vulgar" assumption. Surely it is true that saying a man might be gay was a major insult in that era, a slanderous remark, and it was particularly unthinkable to apply it to a UN Secretary-General.

A plausible proposition, given all the facts, is that Hammarskjöld was a gay man who, at best, was partially aware of his same-sex desires. Unable to fully face and accept this aspect of himself, he arrived at what he considered a principled compromise: he adopted a life of sexual abstinence, rechanneling his sex drive into his work in an effort to escape his inner conflicts while winning widespread professional acclaim. Although this solution was not a healthy one in that it did not lead to his sexual and emotional gratification, it was nevertheless an honorable course of action to Hammarskjöld's way of thinking. He had been taught that homosexuality was a sign of moral degeneracy and that, were he to act on his desires, it would bring suffering to his family, his country, and the United Nations. By renouncing sex, he believed that he was making the proper decision, one that would have no ill effects for anyone but himself, effects he would simply have to endure.

Here it is worth noting that in his private diaries the elusive Swede made reference to a streak of masochism he had discovered in himself. Hammarskjöld took a certain pride in denying himself sexual release; his celibacy provided him with a sense of willfulness, self-discipline, and uniqueness. In this respect, he liked to compare himself to a unicorn and even kept a silver figurine of this mythical animal on his office desk in Manhattan. By choosing to view himself as a mystical singularity rather than an eccentric or social oddity, he seems to have found a way to transform his abstinence into a badge of honor. Hammarskjöld was not the only one to make use of the unicorn motif. Some of his colleagues likewise pointed to the mythical creature whenever the pesky subject of the Secretary-General's sexuality arose, most often by quoting a haiku he once penned regarding the stigma of being single: "Because it never found a mate, men called the unicorn abnormal."[43] These same defenders failed to mention that Hammarskjöld never attempted to find a mate of the opposite sex, and had no wish for a heterosexual union. The argument that he was a bachelor by default, a man who simply could not find a wife, was misleading. Women were drawn to Hammarskjöld, a handsome, cultivated, world-class political figure. It was he who kept them at arms' length. "[E]ven those who greatly admired him sensed this neutrality in him," writes Emery Kelen.[44]

During his tenure at the United Nations, Hammarskjöld became increasingly preoccupied with the martyrdom of Christ. To a very real extent, he identified with Christ's renunciation of earthly desire, single-minded quest for spiritual awareness, altruistic deeds on behalf of humanity, and persecution by society. He further came to believe that, like Christ, he had a unique purpose in life, one that would require him to make personal sacrifices. Thus, in the same way that Hammarskjöld, the college student, insisted that he was too immersed in his studies to pursue a romance, so Hammarskjöld, the statesman, claimed there was no place in his life for an intimate relationship due to his special mission. He even told family and friends it would be unfair of him to marry since he would be unable to provide a wife with the time and attention she deserved. Explaining that his father had inadvertently neglected his mother because of his responsibilities as Prime Minister, Hammarskjöld said he would never subject a woman to a similar situation. Hence, his unshakable refusal to date and wed was now chalked up to the fact that he was a busy international figure who had too much respect for women to court and marry. Throughout the remainder of his life, it was this unconvincing explanation that his friends most often voiced when questioned about his strict bachelorhood.

Of course, it is true that Hammarskjöld really was a very busy man; he made it a point to stay that way. This was easy for him to do since the role of Secretary-General was a truly demanding one for anyone who dared to inhabit it.

GLOBAL PEACEMAKER

As Secretary-General, Hammarskjöld found himself in a position of enormous prestige. At the same time, he was astute enough to recognize the danger inherent in such status, namely, its potential to subvert his efforts to remain true to his welfare-state values and to his concern for the common man. Having grown up in a prominent family, he was familiar with the temptations of power, so he resolved to keep his new circumstances in perspective.

Hammarskjöld's first act as Secretary-General was internal and concerned the excesses of McCarthyism. The Federal Bureau of Investigation, under Trygve Lie's leadership, had been given the green light to set up shop in the UN building, where agents fingerprinted and interrogated all of the nearly 2,000 American employees. The bureau claimed to be looking for "Reds," and any staff member who refused to comply with its inquisition was fired. Despite the existence of constitutional protections against self-incrimination, American employees were not permitted to exercise their Fifth Amendment rights without suffering the consequences. As to the reason for such strong-arm measures, Henry Cabot Lodge, who was the United States Ambassador to the UN, argued that stern actions were necessary to calm public fears that Communist agents might be working within U.S. borders. He failed to mention that the land on which the United Nations stood had been declared international territory.

Only a handful of workers were officially accused of having Communist ties. Far more evident was the plunge in morale caused by the right-wing intrusion; rumors of wholesale firings and forced resignations ran rampant throughout the organization.

During this edgy period the new Secretary-General arrived on the scene, outraged to learn of the FBI presence. Hammarskjöld immediately ordered the federal agents to leave, then drew up a formal edict revoking the bureau's permission to occupy space in the building. He maintained that all UN employees, regardless of nationality, were entitled to a reasonable degree of freedom in thought and action, and that no government, for its own domestic purposes, had the right to enter the organization, intimidate its workers, and demand their dismissals. After making this pronouncement, Hammarskjöld drafted a set of procedures for the organization's use, among them the specific criteria to be used by the UN when deciding if it should investigate one of its staff members and the manner in which the findings should be handled. As a result, he was applauded throughout the organization. His bold intervention buttressed morale for the first time in years.

Hammarskjöld's first major act outside of the UN involved the Korean War, a conflict that had dogged his predecessor and contributed to his downfall. The facts were unequivocal: in 1950, Communist-controlled North Korea invaded South Korea, thereby triggering the bloodshed. Two days later, President Harry Truman ordered the Seventh Fleet into the region ostensibly to prevent the conflict from spreading, while also calling upon the United Nations to help contain the situation. The organization responded by urging sixteen of its member nations to send troops to fortify the American detachment already in Korea. There, these forces, along with the units from the United States, served under General Douglas MacArthur. The war did not abate but instead escalated during the next three years, while discord over the UN's role in the matter intensified within the organization itself.

Then came an astonishing occurrence: within three months of Hammarskjöld's arrival, he helped bring the Korean War to an end by working behind the scenes to assist opposing sides in understanding and appreciating one another's views. He urged that a peace treaty be negotiated by the warring parties, that the conflict not be allowed to drag on until one side achieved a military victory. Antiwar in both outlook and practice, Hammarskjöld was sensitive to the fact that a localized dispute could easily explode into a worldwide maelstrom, a lesson he had learned by observing the onsets of World Wars I and II. As Secretary-General, he had no intention of standing by while another global catastrophe erupted.

China, the United States, and North Korea signed a peace treaty on July 27, 1953. None of these nations were happy about the compromise since none was allowed to "win" the war and thereby lay claim to the disputed territory, but the rest of the world was delighted. Thus, Hammarskjöld had succeeded beyond all expectations in his first international outing, garnering the respect of the UN Security Council, the General Assembly, and heads of state around the globe.

Shortly thereafter, he enjoyed further acclaim in an unrelated realm: the peacetime uses of atomic energy. In 1955, Hammarskjöld set up the first worldwide conference dedicated to exploring such applications, a gathering based in Geneva and attended by scientists from seventy-three nations. Speaking a common language, science, and sharing a common goal, the quest for truth, the participants exchanged formerly secret information that held great promise for such diverse fields as medicine, agriculture, and engineering. Several months later, Hammarskjöld established the International Atomic Energy Agency, with this representing another step forward in the control of nuclear energy. Through such actions, he felt that he was helping to ensure a safer and more peaceful future. A year later, though, he felt less optimistic about the prospects of world harmony when a crisis erupted in northeast Africa.

It occurred in Egypt and involved a dispute over the use of the Suez Canal, a vital piece of real estate and the principal artery between Africa and Asia. A global convention had been held in 1888 culminating in a guarantee that all of the nations of the world would enjoy access to the waterway at all times, with its day-to-day operation being supervised by a collective of nations, France and Britain foremost. For several decades the canal was always accessible to any country that wished to use it. This came to an abrupt halt in 1956, however, when the United States reneged on a deal to furnish Egypt with money to build the Aswan Dam. Egypt, angered by the U.S. denial but determined to go forward with the project, promptly nationalized the Suez Canal, and planned to use the channel's revenue to pay for construction of the dam. Furthermore, it barred Israel, its nemesis, from further use of the waterway.

At once, Hammarskjöld and the UN Security Council initiated a series of closed-door sessions to grapple with the crisis. The result was a resolution calling for Egypt to release its illegal hold on the Canal and reopen it to all seaward traffic. It further called for a group of eighteen nations to henceforth oversee the channel's operation. Egypt consented to the resolution, a turn of events that both surprised and pleased the Secretary-General.

Unfortunately, it was at this delicate moment that Israel decided to launch a surprise attack against Egypt in an invasion that caught Hammarskjöld off guard and caused him to feel betrayed. The next day, he presided over an emergency session of the UN that resulted in a new resolution calling for an immediate cease-fire in the region. France and Britain vetoed the decree, however, then dispatched their own military forces to Egypt and commenced bombing its airfields, aiming to take control of the Suez Canal themselves. Hammarskjöld felt further betrayed by their aggressive deeds.

In a state of exasperation, the UN convened yet again and ordered the Secretary-General to make certain that the cease-fire resolution was carried out. This time, though, it mandated that he create within forty-eight hours a peacekeeping force under the auspices of the United Nations and send it to the region.

With this task in mind, Hammarskjöld assembled a regiment composed largely of soldiers from Scandinavian countries known as the "United Nations Emergency Force." Unlike any other armed force in history, it existed solely to enforce peace. Hammarskjöld then traveled to Egypt to supervise its operation and to meet again with the leaders of the nations entangled in the conflict. Fortunately for everyone involved his actions proved successful. Soon after he arrived in Egypt the UN resolution was honored by all of the countries involved in the dispute, troops were withdrawn, and only the Emergency Force remained.

In the weeks that followed, Hammarskjöld was praised for his accomplishments in preventing the Suez crisis from escalating into a large-scale war. The whole affair had shaken him so deeply, however, that he had nearly resigned. Among other things, he had been injured by media attacks, particularly one in the French press. Angry at the Secretary-General because he had ordered the French military out of the Suez, the article implied that he was gay in an underhanded attempt to exploit the homophobic climate of the era and undermine his reputation. In addition, he still felt the sting of betrayal by Israel, France, and Britain. His trust shattered, he now found it difficult to take seriously these nations' promises. Regardless, Hammarskjöld remained at his post, although embittered and more pessimistic, even cynical, about the prospects of lasting peace in the world.

The statesman felt increasingly burdened by the pressures of his job, the intrusions of the media, and the expectations he placed on himself. To unwind, he read fiction, most notably the works of Thomas Mann and Marcel Proust, as well as the nonfiction of André Gide and Martin Buber. He also listened to Bach's Brandenburg Concertos, nurtured an interest in nature photography, and entertained celebrities at his Park Avenue apartment. Leonard Bernstein, John Steinbeck, and Pablo Cassals were among his guests. He was most content, however, when he was ensconced in a second home he had purchased in a rural area north of Manhattan, where he smoked black cigars and read the verse of Robert Frost. Then, in 1957, an event took place that brought him renewed strength: he was re-elected to a second term as Secretary-General by a unanimous vote of the General Assembly. For the uncertain Swede, it was a pleasant surprise, a much-appreciated vote of confidence signifying that he was performing his job well.

By this point in his UN career, Hammarskjöld had become convinced that a Secretary-General must be a robust, proactive force in world politics, not merely a coordinator of bureaucratic activities, and that both controversy and media attacks come with the territory. He also had come to believe that whenever possible attention should be given to brush-fire conflicts, small regional disputes that, if left unattended, risked mutating into complex wars involving scores of nations. He was resolute also in his conviction that the UN Emergency Force was indispensable in ensuring peace in troubled areas. A few months later he would create another type of UN contingent when the powder-keg that was the Middle East threatened to explode once again.

In this latest episode, a handful of Arab nations having a long history of animosity toward one another began pairing off for a confrontation. The year was 1958. Iraq and Jordan merged to form the Arab Federation while Egypt and Syria combined to create the United Arab Republic. Egypt further wished to add Lebanon to its holdings, so it began sending agitators into that nation's Christian and Moslem sects to fan existing hostilities and incite a civil war. Its plan was to weaken Lebanon internally, then invade it.

Sensing this plot, Lebanon asked the United Nations for assistance in preventing Egyptian subversives from slipping across its borders. Before the UN could act, however, the United States declared its intent to send troops into Lebanon purportedly to protect it. Alarmed by this dangerous turn of events, Hammarskjöld quickly intervened to discourage the American government from going forward with its dubious plan. He explained that an American presence in the Middle East could very well invite a Soviet presence in response, thereby introducing the Cold War conflict into a region already beset with problems of its own. Better the United States and the USSR stay out of the Middle East, he maintained. The United States agreed to back down, at least for the moment.

Shortly thereafter, Hammarskjöld, to make sure the United States stayed away from the region, submitted an innovative plan to the United Nations. The plan called for the formation of a UN "observer force" to be dispatched to Lebanon to guarantee that the nation's borders were not breached. Unlike the Emergency Force sent to the Suez, which was an armed regiment, the observer force would be unarmed. It would exist solely to detect infiltration attempts and report them to the UN and to the world media, thereby exposing Egyptian efforts to incite trouble in Lebanon. Hammarskjöld believed public exposure could be just as effective as an armed confrontation. The United Nations agreed to his plan, and sent to Lebanon a team of 100 men and women, along with aircraft and land vehicles. The contingent soon proved itself effective in patrolling that nation's borders—effective, that is, until another dispute erupted in nearby Iraq a few weeks later.

In this new clash, a revolutionary faction within the Iraqi army overthrew the government and assassinated the king. Worried the same fate might befall Lebanon, Lebanese officials asked the White House for a pledge of protection and the United States responded by sending in the Marines. This hasty action proved problematical, however, in that no real threat existed in Lebanon. The Marines landed on beaches strewn with sunbathers and soft-drink venders. What did happen is that the world railed at the American intervention. Not only did the United States' enemies condemn its potentially destabilizing actions in the troubled hotspot, but its allies did so as well. Even large sections of the Lebanese citizenry opposed the U.S. presence. Within days, international demands were issued insisting that the United States leave Lebanon before the Soviet Union sent its own troops into the region.

It was now that Hammarskjöld intervened a second time. In a formal document, he proposed that both Eastern and Western powers adopt a hands-off policy in the Middle East and respect the Arab nations' right to settle their own disputes. This meant the Americans should leave. He further suggested that the Middle Eastern nations involved in the dispute adopt a policy of nonaggression among themselves, then convene to work out their disagreements in a constructive fashion. Last, he proposed that these same nations devise a collective economic plan that would ultimately enrich the Middle East as a whole. He believed such an endeavor would increase the likelihood of their future cooperation for the sake of the region itself. Hammarskjöld then sent his proposal to Arab leaders to review and amend as necessary. In a remarkable instance of cooperation these officials subsequently submitted a tailored version of the document, known as the "Good Neighbor Policy," to the General Assembly for consideration, which heartily approved it. With this auspicious turn of events, the U.S. Marines left Lebanon, the Middle East returned to a state of relative peace, and Hammarskjöld was applauded yet again for resolving a complicated dispute. By all accounts, he had become the shining star of global politics. Not everyone was delighted by his accomplishments, however. In many instances powerful world leaders, most notably Soviet Premier Nikita Khrushchev and U.S. President John Kennedy, were distinctly displeased by his actions. Hammarskjöld was frequently at odds with both of these men, despite their ersatz embraces for the camera crews. He was most opposed by Khrushchev, though, a fact that would become evident during the Congo affair, the final political crisis of Hammarskjöld's career.

TRAGEDY IN THE CONGO

For several centuries, European colonialism existed in Africa, but this imperialistic system began to collapse in the early to mid-twentieth century when several African nations clamored for the restoration of their freedom. These intrepid nations were successful in their quest. The ensuing retreat of the European powers, notably France, Belgium, and England, was a welcome turn of events, but their abrupt departures were not without consequences. Many fledgling African nations found themselves wholly unprepared to receive their freedom, quite literally, overnight. The leap from political oppression to autonomy was far too sudden.

This was perhaps most clearly the case for the Republic of the Congo, an area the size of Western Europe located in the heart of Africa and a region Belgium had dominated since 1885. This situation came to a halt in the late 1950s when the Congolese people at last rose up in protest, overwhelming the Belgian authorities and forcing the return of their nation's sovereignty. But although Belgium did indeed restore the Congo's freedom, it did not do so completely, instead keeping a firm hold on Katanga Province, the Congo's most mineral-rich region. Furthermore, to ensure its continued access to this lucrative area, Belgium began pressuring the province's leader, Moise Tshombe, to engineer its secession from the Congo. Widely considered a pawn of the Belgian government, Tshombe was despised by the Congolese people, and understandably so, since his actions hurt their nation.

Katanga Province provided what little wealth the nation enjoyed, revenue the Congo desperately needed. Certainly poverty was rampant and the prospects for future enrichment, bleak. Despite a population of ten million, in the entire country there were no Congolese physicians, merely a handful of lawyers and engineers, one university with less than two dozen students, and fourteen college graduates. By all accounts, the Congo was struggling. Sadly, within two weeks of receiving its liberty the nation began to disintegrate economically, politically, and socially. During the summer of 1960, tribal disputes broke out in the bush, Congolese nationalists attacked those Belgians who remained inside the country, and the wrath of the Congolese people toward Moise Tshombe and his minions in Katanga Province threatened to explode into all-out war. The situation worsened when the Belgian government sent in troops to protect the handful of Belgians who remained there, as well as to safeguard its financial interests in the Katanga region. Now that the Congo was a republic, such military action constituted foreign aggression. Patrice Lumumba, the Congo's new Prime Minister, contacted the UN and petitioned Hammarskjöld to intervene. He asked the Secretary-General to dispatch the Emergency Force to protect his country from the European troops.

Believing the request to be a worthy one, Hammarskjöld took the matter before the Security Council, which authorized the use of UN forces in keeping peace in the region. This meant the Belgian military would have no choice but to leave, since the UN would be assuming responsibility for protecting all of the people in the Congo, Belgian as well as Congolese.

Hammarskjöld arranged for 20,000 troops from Sweden, Canada, and several African nations to go to the Congo. He also put together a substantial aid package to help the faltering republic get back on its feet, ensuring that 1,000 Congolese citizens would be enrolled in vocational training programs. The package also called for UN appointees to temporarily operate the nation's hospitals, airports, and communication systems, and authorized scores of teachers to be sent to the region, along with 100 medical specialists from twenty nations. It further stipulated that thousands of tons of food be distributed to the citizenry. These actions, moreover, did help stabilize the country, at least until Prime Minister Lumumba threw a wrench into the effort by railing against Hammarskjöld and the UN presence in the Congo.

Lumumba had become disenchanted with the UN Emergency Force. He had wrongly assumed that its principal function would be to protect his position as Prime Minister. When he discovered that the Emergency Force was genuinely neutral and was in the Congo expressly to keep the peace rather than serve as his political bodyguard, he denounced Hammarskjöld and told the Emergency Force to leave. He then asked the Soviet Union for assistance, knowing this would alienate the West and win favor in the East.

Shortly after Lumumba shifted his allegiance to the USSR, Khrushchev showed up at the United Nations in Manhattan and demanded that Hammarskjöld resign. Khrushchev's mandate fell on deaf ears. The UN member nations were aware that the USSR, while pretending to hold the Congo's interests close to its heart, had its own designs on the neophyte nation, as well as on several of its neighbors. They knew the Soviet Union hoped to install Communist governments in them, since such dominance in Africa, in combination with its influence in those Asian and European countries it had already subjugated, would provide it with a majority vote in the United Nations. They were further aware that Khrushchev believed Hammarskjöld was standing in the way of the Soviet plan. Accordingly, they voted 70-0 for the Swede to remain at his post, a turn of events that infuriated the Soviet leader. However, this was not the end of the story.

Several months later, the USSR tried again to undermine Hammarskjöld's authority when Prime Minister Lumumba was assassinated in the Congo. Predictably, the Soviet government blamed Hammarskjöld for the murder and began staging protests against him. In one such melee in Paris, a spectacle ostensibly orchestrated by Soviet agitators, French students took to the streets, shouting "Hang Hammarskjöld."[45] Similar eruptions occurred in other world capitals as well. Hammarskjöld refused to capitulate, instead redoubling his efforts to ensure peace in the tumultuous Congo and pressing for its economic advancement. He also remained intent on keeping the Soviet Union and the United States out of Africa, just as he had been determined to keep them away from the Middle East conflict.

With remarkable foresight, Hammarskjöld began laying the groundwork for the establishment of UN secretariats, administrative units put in place to oversee the UN's technical, economic, and social development programs. These secretariats were to be located in several new African nations, including the Congo. His plan was to help these countries become economically self-sufficient so they could better preserve their political autonomy. Naturally, this displeased many leaders, both Eastern and Western, who hoped to befriend these needy nations for their own purposes.

By early 1961, UN peacekeeping forces had managed to bring the violence in the Congo under control in spite of a cadre of snipers who persisted in firing at UN workers and their aircraft. The main problem centered on Belgian instigators who were still living in Katanga Province and urging Moise Tshombe to keep it isolationist so Belgium could continue enjoying access to its minerals. It was at this time that Hammarskjöld sent a message to Tshombe advising him to expel these instigants and participate in talks with the Congo's leadership for the sake of the entire Congo Basin. He believed reuniting Katanga Province with the Congo would be in the long-term interests of the region. Although Tshombe disagreed at first, several months later he agreed to meet with him about the matter.

With this in mind, Hammarskjöld flew to the Congo in September 1961, arriving in the capital city of Léopoldville and checking into a hotel. His plan was to hold discussions with the leadership of the

Congo about UN aid, then fly to the border town of Ndola to meet with Moise Tshombe. Death, however, was on his mind. Only a few weeks before, Hammarskjöld had felt compelled to make a will, and during his last night in Léopoldville, he had read a book about the Crucifixion. His journal entries, as well as the recollections of colleagues, further reveal that Hammarskjöld believed he was destined to die in a moment of self-sacrifice. Tragically, his plane did indeed crash the following night, cutting short his life and stunning the world.

Postscript

In the days and weeks following Hammarskjöld's death, memorial services were held around the globe. Among the more prominent services was the one staged by his grief-stricken colleagues in Manhattan. World leaders expressed their sorrow, too, among them President John F. Kennedy, who declared that the illustrious Swede would forever be "treasured high among the peacemakers of history."[46] Those in Hammarskjöld's homeland, where his remains lay in state, also paid their respects, with 8,000 citizens filing past his flag-draped coffin in the city of Uppsala, while another quarter-million attended an open-air ceremony in Stockholm. As the masses stood in silence, flags representing all of the UN member nations fluttered in the wind as two military bands performed Scandinavian hymns.

Such tributes continued after Hammarskjöld's body was interred. In the succeeding months, public buildings, scholarships, and endowments were named in his honor, while the Swedish Royal Academy awarded him a posthumous Nobel Peace Prize. Universities which had recognized his unprecedented accomplishments during his lifetime continued to acknowledge them after his death. Hammarskjöld collected honorary degrees from Oxford, Columbia, Yale, Johns Hopkins, Princeton, and Harvard Universities, among other institutions. In addition, he was hailed in death by the same Eastern and Western leaders who had sought to impugn his reputation in life. His name would forever remain synonymous with peace, probity, and perseverance. He was further praised for the innovations he had brought to the United Nations itself.

Among other advancements, Hammarskjöld had transformed the role of Secretary-General into one of true leadership, imbued with the power to act independently in political crises wherever they might arise. He had also demonstrated the importance of interceding swiftly in local skirmishes to prevent them from escalating into all-out wars. He had created UN peacekeeping units, most notably the armed Emergency Force and the unarmed "peacekeeping presences," which furnished the UN with a direct, physical role in the world's hotspots. As if this were not enough, he had personally intervened, and successfully so, in major disputes in the Far East and Middle East, as well as working diligently to prevent Cold War elements from annihilating one another. He had further ensured that these same elements did not infect other continents with their potentially lethal quarrel. Moreover, he had brought attention to the plight of persecuted ethnic minorities around the world. By all accounts, his tenure as Secretary-General had been a triumphant one.

Yet Hammarskjöld the man had been a study in contrasts. A proponent of open communication in political affairs, he went to great lengths to withhold even minor details of his personal life from his acquaintances, not to mention the press. Perhaps his paradoxical nature is best illustrated by his rather obvious sexual conflict and the way in which he dealt with it. As noted, Hammarskjöld was arguably a gay man who was unable to fully accept himself as such. Instead of taking steps to reconcile himself with his sexual orientation, he evidently lived out his days in abstinence, a condition that frustrated and depressed him deeply. Yet side by side with his inability to understand and accept his apparent homosexuality was his uncanny capacity to thrust himself into convoluted political firestorms in diverse regions of the world and devise creative solutions that benefitted all of the parties involved. Thus, while he could not resolve his own internal conflicts, he forged a stellar career by settling complex external disputes, and this, more than anything else, captures the essence of the elusive and enigmatic Dag Hammarskjöld: a tormented man whose flight into his work, while leaving him emotionally and sexually bereft, allowed millions of others to enjoy a more meaningful, more confident future.

NOTES

1. Levine, Israel, *Champion of World Peace: Dag Hammarskjöld* (New York: Julian Messner, 1962, p. 179).

2. Kelen, Emery, *Hammarskjöld* (New York: Putnam, 1966, p. 30).

3. Ibid.

4. Hershey, Burnet, *Soldier of Peace: Dag Hammarskjöld* (Chicago: Encyclopedia Britannica Press, 1961, p. 30).

5. Agnes Hammarskjöld, in Hershey, *Soldier of Peace,* p. 34.

6. Kelen, *Hammarskjöld,* p. 29.

7. Ibid., p. 35.

8. Levine, *Champion of World Peace,* p. 19.

9. Stolpe, Sven, *Dag Hammarskjöld: A Spiritual Portrait* (New York: Charles Scribner's Sons, 1966, p. 17).

10. Dag Hammarskjöld, in Van Dusen, Henry, *Dag Hammarskjöld: The Statesman and His Faith* (New York: Harper & Row, 1964, p. 15).

11. Jarl Hjalmarson, in Hershey, *Soldier of Peace,* p. 39.

12. Fussell, Paul, *The Great War and Modern Memory* (Oxford: Oxford University Press, 1975/2000, p. 3).

13. Wells, H. G., The Idea of a League of Nations. *The Atlantic Monthly* (January, 1919). *The Atlantic Monthly Online* Web site <www.theatlantic.com/issues/19jan/leag119.htm>, p. 4.

14. Hjalmar Hammarskjöld, in Stolpe, *Dag Hammarskjöld,* p. 20.

15. Hershey, *Soldier of Peace,* p. 39.

16. Levine, *Champion of World Peace,* pp. 28-29.

17. Hershey, *Soldier of Peace,* p. 44.

18. Stolpe, *Dag Hammarskjöld,* p. 31.

19. Auden, in Hammarskjöld, Dag, *Markings* (New York: Alfred Knopf, 1964/1981).

20. Dag Hammarskjöld, in Van Dusen, *Dag Hammarskjöld,* p. 26.

21. Cowan, Thomas, *Gay Men and Women Who Enriched the World* (New Canaan, CT: Mulvey Books, 1988, p. 155).

22. Van Dusen, *Dag Hammarskjöld,* p. 23.

23. Hjalmar Hammarskjöld, in Levine, *Champion of World Peace,* p. 26.

24. Hammarskjöld, *Markings,* p. 8.

25. Dag Hammarskjöld, in Van Dusen, *Dag Hammarskjöld,* p. 55.

26. Hershey, *Soldier of Peace,* p. 51.

27. Harrington, Michael, *Socialism* (New York: Bantam Books, 1972, p. 238).

28. Dag Hammarskjöld, in Urquhart, Brian, *Hammarskjöld* (New York: Alfred Knopf, 1973, p. 22).

29. Sten Söderberg, in Stolpe, *Dag Hammarskjöld,* p. 25.

30. Van Dusen, *Dag Hammarskjöld,* p. 17.

31. Dag Hammarskjöld, in Van Dusen, *Dag Hammarskjöld,* p. 60.

32. Stolpe, *Dag Hammarskjöld,* p. 48.

33. Wigforss, in Levine, *Champion of World Peace,* p. 49.

34. Dag Hammarskjöld, in Levine, *Champion of World Peace,* p. 51.

35. Hammarskjöld, in UN document (2001, p. 3).

36. In Kelen, *Hammarskjöld,* p. 153.

37. Green, Richard, *The "Sissy Boy" Syndrome and the Development of Homosexuality* (New Haven, CT: Yale University Press, 1987).

38. Löfström, Jan, ed., *Scandinavian Homosexualities: Essays on Gay and Lesbian Studies* (Binghamton, NY: Harrington Park Press, 1998, p. 6).

39. Ibid., p. 6).

40. Auden, in Hammarskjöld, *Markings,* p. xi.

41. Hammarskjöld, *Markings,* p. 59.
42. Urquhart, *Hammarskjöld,* p. 27.
43. Hammarskjöld, *Markings,* p. 193.
44. Kelen, *Hammarskjöld,* p. 155.
45. Anonymous, Lumumba's Legacy: Trouble All Over. *Life Magazine* (February 24, 1961): 17.
46. Kennedy, in Levine, *Champion of World Peace,* p. 182.

REFERENCES

Anonymous (February 24, 1961). Lumumba's legacy: Trouble all over. *Life Magazine,* pp. 16-21.
Anonymous (2001). *Dag Hammarskjöld: Second United Nations Secretary-General.* United Nations Web site <www.un.org/Depts/dhl/dag/time1953/htm>.
Cowan, Thomas (1988). *Gay Men and Women Who Enriched the World.* New Canaan, Connecticut: Mulvey Books.
Fussell, Paul (1975/2000). *The Great War and Modern Memory.* Oxford: Oxford University Press.
Green, Richard (1987). *The "Sissy Boy" Syndrome and the Development of Homosexuality.* New Haven, CT: Yale University Press.
Hammarskjöld, Dag (1964/1981). *Markings.* New York: Alfred Knopf.
Harrington, Michael (1970). *Socialism.* New York: Bantam Books.
Hershey, Burnet (1961). *Soldier of Peace: Dag Hammarskjöld.* Chicago: Encyclopedia Britannica Press.
Kelen, Emery (1966). *Hammarskjöld.* New York: Putnam.
Levine, Israel (1962). *Champion of World Peace: Dag Hammarskjöld.* New York: Julian Messner.
Löfström, Jan (Editor) (1998). *Scandinavian Homosexualities: Essays on Gay and Lesbian Studies.* Binghamton, NY: Harrington Park Press.
Stolpe, Sven (1965/1966). *Dag Hammarskjöld: A Spiritual Portrait.* New York: Charles Scribner's Sons.
Urquhart, Brian (1973). *Hammarskjöld.* New York: Alfred Knopf.
Van Dusen, Henry (1964). *Dag Hammarskjöld: The Statesman and His Faith.* New York: Harper & Row.
Wells, H. G. (January, 1919). The idea of a league of nations. *The Atlantic Monthly. The Atlantic Monthly Online* Web site <www.theatlantic.com/issues/19jan/leag119.htm>.

Epilogue

The three illustrious men whose lives were revisited in the course of this book were very much alike in certain respects. They all shared persistent insecurities of an intensity well beyond that experienced by the average person.

Author Glenway Wescott suffered from a painful lack of self-esteem, having little confidence in himself as an author. Because he was unsure of his writing talent, he endured decades-long bouts of writer's block, which, in turn, further eroded his self-esteem and prolonged his inability to create. Wescott was his own worst enemy when it came to his role as author.

Composer Aaron Copland likewise suffered certain insecurities, among them a self-consciousness about his physical appearance. He was convinced that men sometimes became romantically involved with him for reasons other than amorous ones. He was also uneasy with the anger and disapproval of other people and abhorred ugly scenes. For this reason, he avoided conflict as much as possible, and when he did find himself in antagonistic circumstances, tried strenuously to remain calm and composed.

Dag Hammarskjöld was riddled with anxieties as well as being inordinately uncomfortable discussing personal matters with others. He routinely rebuffed reporters' queries about his day-to-day existence and changed the subject whenever his friends asked about his personal life. He also recoiled from direct confrontation with others, rarely raised his voice, and shied away from asserting himself even in benign social situations. Indeed, this was a UN Secretary-General who was so unwilling to impose on his colleagues' hospitality that he once spent Christmas with the janitors in the basement of the United Nations building rather than dine with his co-workers in their homes during the seasonal holiday.

Given these features of Wescott, Copland, and Hammarskjöld, one cannot help being impressed by their adeptness in their careers and public lives. Each man, despite serious self-doubt, also possessed self-awareness, including a knowledge of the ways in which his insecurity manifested itself in his life. He was therefore able to surmount, or at least sidestep, his inner uncertainties, thereby continuing to move forward professionally.

Another feature shared by these men was an alternative sexuality, alternative in the sense that it was contrary to the norms of the conservative and conformist times in which they lived. Furthermore, each man experienced and expressed his sexuality in his own unique fashion, in some cases with very productive results.

Glenway Wescott lived an open and adventurous gay life, sometimes in the form of threesomes with other men. He also wrote a graphic account of one of his homoerotic encounters and helped sexologist Alfred Kinsey prepare a pioneering book that presented important new information about homosexuality in American society. By any measure, Wescott made a tangible contribution to gay life in his era.

Aaron Copland favored serial monogamy with gay musicians and composers. He believed that his sexual disposition affected his art, that his attraction to, and affection for, other men informed his musical compositions in a subtle but distinctive fashion. His was a love that permeated the opera *The Tender Land,* among other notable works.

Dag Hammarskjöld, by comparison, appears to have suppressed and sublimated his sexual energies, channeling his erotic impulses into his work as a statesman. Thus, in this rare and intriguing case, a man's denial, rather than acceptance, of his apparent same-sex desires yielded enormous dividends for humankind.

From the foregoing, it is evident that the sexualities of Wescott, Copland, and Hammarskjöld were instrumental in their careers. Had these men been mainstream heterosexuals, some of their most meaningful accomplishments might never have become realities.

Last, all three figures successfully challenged the popular myth that men and women of principle who conduct themselves with empathy and civility invariably find themselves trounced by the more ruthless breed of career climber. The fact is, Wescott, Copland, and Hammarskjöld reached the pinnacle of success without being overtaken by unscrupulous contenders. They also did so without forfeiting their own humanity along the way. Rarely, if ever, were they accused of being deceitful or manipulative or of riding roughshod over their colleagues. Quite the opposite, the three earned the longstanding admiration of even their staunchest adversaries. Furthermore, their regard for those around them did not wane as they gained great fame. If anything, their complaisance increased as their accomplishments attracted worldwide recognition and respect. Wescott, Copland, and Hammarskjöld were exceptional figures of the twentieth century, brilliant men of talent and integrity from whom much can be learned today as we enter the new millennium.

Further Reading

For readers who wish to explore further the men and works discussed in this book, the following sources are recommended:

Glenway Wescott

Phelps, Robert and Rosco, Jerry (Eds.) (1990). *Continual Lessons: The Journals of Glenway Wescott, 1937-1955*. New York: Farrar, Straus and Giroux.
Rosco, Jerry (2002). *Glenway Wescott, Personally: A Biography*. Madison, Wisconsin: University of Wisconsin Press.
Wescott, Glenway (1962). *Images of Truth*. New York: Harper & Row.
Wescott, Glenway (2001, 1940). *The Pilgrim Hawk*. New York: New York Review Books.

Aaron Copland

Copland, Aaron and Perlis, Vivian (1984). *Copland: 1900 Through 1942*. New York: St. Martin's/Griffin.
Copland, Aaron and Perlis, Vivian (1989). *Copland: After 1943*. New York: St. Martin's/Griffin.
Dickinson, Peter (Ed.) (2002). *Copland Connotations: Studies and Interviews*. Woodbridge, England: Boydell Press.
Pollack, Howard (1999). *Aaron Copland: The Life and Work of an Uncommon Man*. New York: Henry Holt.

Dag Hammarskjöld

Hammarskjöld, Dag (1964/198). *Markings*. New York: Alfred Knopf.
Little, Marie-Noëlle (Ed.) (2001). *The Poet and the Diplomat: The Correspondence of Dag Hammarskjöld and Alexis Leger*. Syracuse, New York: Syracuse University Press.
Stolpe, Sven (1965/1966). *Dag Hammarskjöld: A Spiritual Portrait*. New York: Charles Scribner's Sons.
Urquhart, Brian (1973). *Hammarskjöld*. New York: Alfred Knopf.

Index

Order a copy of this book with this form or online at:
http://www.haworthpress.com/store/product.asp?sku=5401

NOBLE LIVES

Biographical Portraits of Three Remarkable Gay Men— Glenway Wescott, Aaron Copland, and Dag Hammarskjöld

_____in hardbound at $39.95 (ISBN: 1-56023-294-3)

_____in softbound at $17.95 (ISBN: 1-56023-545-4)

Or order online and use special offer code HEC25 in the shopping cart.

COST OF BOOKS_____

POSTAGE & HANDLING_____
*(US: $4.00 for first book & $1.50
for each additional book)*
*(Outside US: $5.00 for first book
& $2.00 for each additional book)*

SUBTOTAL_____

IN CANADA: ADD 7% GST_____

STATE TAX_____
*(NJ, NY, OH, MN, CA, IL, IN, PA, & SD
residents, add appropriate local sales tax)*

FINAL TOTAL_____
*(If paying in Canadian funds,
convert using the current
exchange rate, UNESCO
coupons welcome)*

☐ **BILL ME LATER:** (Bill-me option is good on US/Canada/Mexico orders only; not good to jobbers, wholesalers, or subscription agencies.)
☐ Check here if billing address is different from shipping address and attach purchase order and billing address information.

Signature_____

☐ **PAYMENT ENCLOSED: $_____**

☐ **PLEASE CHARGE TO MY CREDIT CARD.**

☐ Visa ☐ MasterCard ☐ AmEx ☐ Discover
☐ Diner's Club ☐ Eurocard ☐ JCB

Account # _____

Exp. Date_____

Signature_____

Prices in US dollars and subject to change without notice.

NAME_____

INSTITUTION_____

ADDRESS_____

CITY_____

STATE/ZIP_____

COUNTRY_____ COUNTY (NY residents only)_____

TEL_____ FAX_____

E-MAIL_____

May we use your e-mail address for confirmations and other types of information? ☐ Yes ☐ No
We appreciate receiving your e-mail address and fax number. Haworth would like to e-mail or fax special discount offers to you, as a preferred customer. **We will never share, rent, or exchange your e-mail address or fax number.** We regard such actions as an invasion of your privacy.

Order From Your Local Bookstore or Directly From
The Haworth Press, Inc.
10 Alice Street, Binghamton, New York 13904-1580 • USA
TELEPHONE: 1-800-HAWORTH (1-800-429-6784) / Outside US/Canada: (607) 722-5857
FAX: 1-800-895-0582 / Outside US/Canada: (607) 771-0012
E-mailto: orders@haworthpress.com

For orders outside US and Canada, you may wish to order through your local
sales representative, distributor, or bookseller.
For information, see http://haworthpress.com/distributors

(Discounts are available for individual orders in US and Canada only, not booksellers/distributors.)
PLEASE PHOTOCOPY THIS FORM FOR YOUR PERSONAL USE.
http://www.HaworthPress.com   BOF04